THE ILLUSTRATED GUIDE TO
PREGNANCY
AND BIRTH

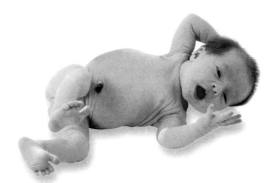

THE ILLUSTRATED GUIDE TO
PREGNANCY AND BIRTH

TINA OTTE

PHOTOGRAPHY BY LISA TROCCHI

AUTHOR'S ACKNOWLEDGMENTS

To all the many women and men who have taught me so much by sharing the most intimate
experience of childbirth with me, I thank you.
I wish to thank my dearest friends Charisse and Rob Otty and their sons for gracing many
pages of this book. Thank you for sharing your experience of
pregnancy, childbirth and early parenting.
To the many mothers who allowed us to share their pregnancies, moments of birth and
the time afterwards, and to the doctors who allowed us to photograph the procedures and
operations that are in this book, thank you. Specifically, I would like to thank Zan Giemre,
Wendy Coetzee and baby Kira, Michelle de Laat, Bradley Kahn and baby Joshua, Nicky Austin,
and Melissa and Sandy Stephenson.
Sincere thanks to the staff of various hospitals for allowing us to capture many of the
photographs in this book, especially the birth photographs.
Lisa Trocchi, thank you for teaching me so much about photography, and for
your patience and superb photographic skills.
Professor Justus Hofmeyr, who has checked the contents of this book, you will never know
how honored I am to have someone of your standing contribute to this book.
Thanks to the publishers, and to my editors, Sally Rutherford and Jenny Sutcliffe, for all your work,
patience and time in taking my words and making them 'reader friendly'. What would I have
done without you? A special word of thanks to Petal Palmer, who designed every page
of this book. You are truly a master of your craft.
Finally to my family – my husband Ralph and daughters Natasha and Nicole.
Thank you for the many cups of tea, the dinners, and the space you gave me when I needed
peace and quiet to write. Thank you for putting up with my moods and
for being there when I needed reassurance and encouragement.
Thank you for believing in me.

"A woman giving birth to a child has pain because her time has come; but when her baby is born
she forgets the anguish, because of her joy that a child is born into the world."
JOHN 16 V 21 (NIV)

FOREWORD

This is a book for parents and prospective parents – for all of us who face with courage and
trepidation the deep joys and pain of parenthood.

Life in modern times is not straightforward. Medical techniques have greatly improved the safety
of childbirth, but at a price: as responsibility for our health is taken over by medical personnel,
we lose some of the sense of strength and belief in ourselves that is vital to our ability
to become confident and resourceful parents.

Each of us is ultimately responsible for our own health and life, and we must therefore hold
onto our autonomy and our right to make choices and decisions. Although we can expect expert
advice and help from health professionals, we cannot expect them all to share our
personal beliefs, approaches to life and priorities.

This book will enrich our understanding of the processes and issues of childbirth. With
understanding comes confidence in our own ability to make the best decisions, to face with
courage the challenges, to overcome the setbacks without blame or regret, and to experience to the
fullest extent the overwhelming joys and wonders of our part in the creation of new human life.

G. JUSTUS HOFMEYR M.R.C.O.G.
Chief Specialist/Professor, Department of Obstetrics and Gynecology,
Coronation Hospital and the University of the Witwatersrand

INTRODUCTION

I am honored and proud to have been given this opportunity to write a book on pregnancy and birth from a childbirth educator's point of view. Becoming a mother for the first time was a great joy, but also involved dramatic change as well as unforeseen anxiety. I struggled to come to terms with the way in which I had delivered as well as with feelings of inadequacy as I battled with breastfeeding and early mothering. It had never entered my mind for a moment that I would have these feelings, as my husband and I had planned the pregnancy and looked forward to the birth with much excitement and joy. I had believed that 'mothering' would come naturally and that I would automatically know what to do at every crisis. Instead I discovered that, although women are natural nurturers, mothering is a skill that is acquired 'on the job'. I felt that if I, as a trained nurse and midwife, could be so ill-prepared for the task of being a mother, there must be many other women out there who feel the same way I did, if not worse! My concern for other women approaching this very important life event motivated me to enter the fascinating world of childbirth education. I have never looked back. Through teaching and sharing the experience of childbirth and parenting with hundreds of expectant parents I have not only 'healed' myself of the doubt I experienced, but have helped to guide others towards a satisfying birth experience. This has been a true privilege.

I have written this book honestly and realistically. My aim is to inform women about the broader issues of pregnancy and birth, and with this illustrated book I hope to make the information easily accessible and simple to understand. I hope women who read it will realize that they need to take responsibility for their bodies and their babies, and that preparing for birth and parenting is as important as preparing for any other occasion where they may have influence over the lives of others. Pregnancy and birth are not about handing over responsibility to your doctor or midwife: it is up to you to educate yourself about all your options so that you can choose the ones that best suit you. The more you know about all aspects of pregnancy and birth, the more empowered you will be to enjoy this life event on your own terms.

I believe, too, in a holistic view of pregnancy. It is not just the physiological changes that are important: your state of mind, your diet and your general well-being have an enormous influence on how you feel about and cope with your pregnancy. A good diet and appropriate exercise also contribute to a healthy mother and baby, and will give you the energy to handle the challenges of pregnancy and birth in a positive way. I hope that the information and advice contained in this book will help you to adjust all aspects of your life in order to make the most of your own experience.

Becoming a parent is all about courage and love. I wish you good luck and much joy!

Tina Otte

TINA OTTE

CONTENTS

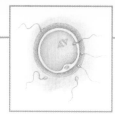

CHAPTER 1

BECOMING PREGNANT

The First Stages

W hen you decide to become a parent you are making one of the most important decisions of your life, so it is vital that both would-be parents are fully prepared for what lies ahead of them. But being able to plan your pregnancy in advance, consider your options and make informed decisions about your body and your pregnancy will help you prepare for the experience with confidence – and help promote a healthy lifestyle both during your pregnancy and after it.

It is a good idea to consult your doctor before you become pregnant, both to make sure that you are in good physical condition and to discuss any changes it may be necessary to make in your lifestyle. Keep a diary of your menstrual cycle, too, so that you are sure of the date of your last menstrual period.

ARE YOU FIT FOR PREGNANCY?

Preconception care increases the chances of having an enjoyable pregnancy, an easier birth and a healthy baby – and remember that your baby is likely to develop in your womb for several weeks before you realize that you are pregnant. So run through this checklist, and take the appropriate action before you try to conceive.

Choosing to become parents is perhaps the most important decision you will ever make, so give yourself time to make sure that you are fully informed about all aspects of pregnancy and birth and in good health before trying to conceive.

- Do you smoke, drink alcohol or take any drugs that have not been prescribed by a doctor? If so, stop – at least three months before trying to conceive.
- Are you taking any prescription drugs? If so, tell your doctor that you are intending to try to become pregnant. Don't stop taking prescribed drugs without consulting your doctor.
- Are you up to date with your immunizations, for German measles (rubella), for example? Such immunizations will not be given while you are pregnant.
- Would it be wise for you to be tested for any sexually transmitted disease?
- How safe is your workplace and home environment? Are you exposed to anything that is potentially harmful? Avoid toxic sprays and vapors, gasoline fumes, over-hot baths, cat feces (which may carry a parasite called toxoplasma); also wash hands after touching raw meat.
- How fit are you? Pregnancy puts extra strain on muscles and joints as the ligaments that stabilize them slacken, so it's worthwhile starting an exercise program.
- Do you eat a healthy, balanced diet? If not, change your eating habits (see page 27).
- Do you take folic acid supplements? If not, start now (see page 28).
- Do any medical conditions run in your family? If so, you should consider seeking genetic counseling.

CREATING A NEW LIFE

Conception – the moment at which a new life is created – occurs when a male sperm pierces the wall of a female egg and the nuclei of the two cells fuse. But this rather bald, flat statement disguises a remarkable sequence of events, and an understanding of them – and of how the baby develops subsequently – will help you anticipate the changes that your body will make during pregnancy with pleasure.

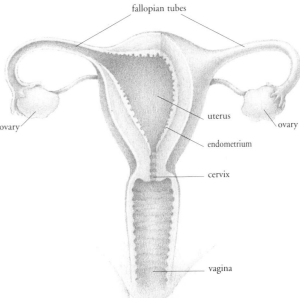

Female *reproductive anatomy.*

The internal female genitalia comprise the vagina, the uterus, or womb, and the two fallopian tubes and ovaries. The vagina is a fibromuscular tube about three inches (7.5 cm) long that is very elastic, allowing it to stretch around a man's penis during intercourse and around the baby's head during the second stage of labor. The uterus is a hollow, muscular organ, shaped like a flattened pear, that sits behind the bladder and in front of the rectum. It has two parts: the upper one, the body, and the lower one, the cervix. The latter is made up of fibrous connective tissue and protrudes into the vagina.

The two fallopian tubes lie one on each side of the womb within the folds of the broad ligament, which is one of the womb's supports, and open out from the womb to extend outward and backward toward the ovaries.

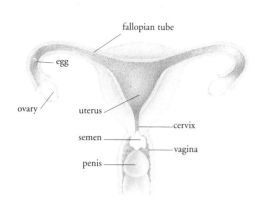

After ovulation *the egg moves into the fallopian tube, heading toward the uterus.*

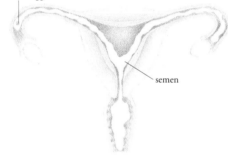

Semen travels *via the cervix and uterus into the fallopian tubes, where one sperm fertilizes the egg.*

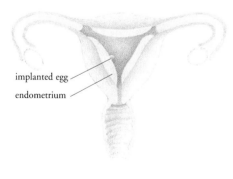

The fertilized egg *moves into the uterus and implants in the uterine lining, where it develops into a fetus.*

The ovaries, one of which is on each side of the womb, are the female sex glands. Their main function is to produce egg cells (ova), but after having been stimulated by hormones from the pituitary gland during puberty, they start to secrete the hormones estrogen and progesterone: it is these hormones that trigger the physical changes that take place in women during adolescence, such as the growth of breasts and body hair.

The moment of conception

The first step in the sequence that results in the creation of the new life is ovulation, the process by which an egg is released from one of the ovaries. This usually occurs on about the 14th day of the typical 28-day menstrual cycle, and once the egg has been released it can be fertilized at any time during the next 12 to 24 hours. Rhythmic contractions of the fallopian tubes, together with the movement of minute hairs, called cilia, gently waft the egg along towards the uterus.

At the same time, the cervix secretes an alkaline mucus that attracts sperm. About 300 million sperm are deposited high up in the vagina when a man ejaculates, but they then have to travel through the cervix, into the uterus and then up into the fallopian tubes, and large numbers die in the course of the journey. The sperm become mature on the way, and acquire the capacity to release an enzyme that is needed to soften the jelly-like inner coating of the egg. It takes large numbers of sperm to soften this coating, but eventually one penetrates the egg, after which the egg's membrane is sealed to prevent the entry of any further sperm. Then the nucleus of the successful sperm fuses with the nucleus of the egg to form a single fertilized cell, called a zygote: a new life.

Boy or girl?

Each fertilized egg contains 46 chromosomes, half of which come from the mother's egg cell and half from the father's sperm. Chromosomes are tiny, thread-like structures that each carry thousands of genes – it is these that determine the characteristics that the baby will inherit from his or her parents, such as hair and eye color and blood type. Two of the chromosomes are sex chromosomes, of which one comes from the mother and one from the father: the one from the mother is always the X chromosome, but the one from the father may be either an X or a Y chromosome – so it is the father who determines the sex of the baby. If the egg is fertilized by a sperm containing an X chromosome, the baby will be a girl (XX). If the sperm contains a Y chromosome then the baby will be a boy (XY).

How are twins formed?

Twins occur spontaneously about once in every 80 pregnancies, though your chance of having twins increases if either you or your partner has a family history of twins or if you have taken infertility drugs.

In around two-thirds of cases, twins are 'fraternal', which means that each baby comes from a different egg, each one having been fertilized by a different sperm. Such twins can be of the opposite sex and are as likely to resemble each other as any brother or sister is – they just happen to have been conceived at the same time. And because fraternal twins are two distinct embryos, each twin has its own placenta and its own amniotic sac.

Identical twins, on the other hand, come about when one fertilized egg splits into two separate cells, each of which develops into a baby. Because they originate from the same cell each baby has the same genes, is of the same sex and looks alike. Such twins usually have their own amniotic sac, but may share a placenta.

Twins are conceived in just over one percent of pregnancies.

SIGNS OF PREGNANCY

The earliest and most reliable sign of pregnancy for a woman who has a regular menstrual cycle is a missed period. Other signs of pregnancy are:

◆ your breasts feel full, heavy and tender and the areola becomes darker;
◆ you urinate frequently, especially at night;
◆ you may feel nauseous and even vomit during the day;
◆ you experience an increase in vaginal discharge but there is no irritation;
◆ you suddenly become averse to certain foods, and sometimes to tobacco smoke;
◆ you feel 'full' in your lower abdomen and tired and drowsy.

PREGNANCY TESTS

A hormone called human chorionic gonadotrophin (HCG) is only produced during pregnancy, and a pregnancy test checks your urine – or, on very rare occasions, your blood – for its presence. Home urine-testing kits are readily available, and a sample should be taken from the middle of a stream of urine passed first thing in the morning. A positive result is almost always correct, though a negative result is less reliable, and you should ask your doctor to confirm it.

HOW WILL I FEEL?

Most women are ecstatically happy when they discover that they are pregnant, and are thrilled to anticipate the physical changes that occur during pregnancy and prepare to enjoy them. Sometimes, however, women are scared about what lies ahead of them and dismayed at the way their bodies will change – especially if the pregnancy has not been planned. If this is how you feel, remember that you will have nine months to come to terms with your pregnancy. Attending prenatal classes from the beginning will put you in touch with other pregnant women who are undergoing similar experiences, and you will be able to share your feelings about the changes that are taking place within you. Take your time to prepare yourself, your partner, your family and your home for your future with your new baby: there will be extra pressures, but also many extra blessings.

To work out your expected date of delivery, look up the first day of your last menstrual period in the month in bold print. Then look at the date immediately to the right of that to see your due date. (For example, if your last period started on April 13th, your due date is January 18th.)

CALCULATING YOUR DUE DATE

Pregnancy is calculated from the first day of your last period and lasts an average of 280 days, or 40 weeks. Your expected date of delivery (EDD) is an approximate date: only five percent of babies arrive on their due date, but two-thirds are born within ten days of their due date. In fact, your baby may be born at any time from three weeks before the EDD to two weeks after it.

CALCULATING YOUR EXPECTED DATE OF DELIVERY

JAN	OCT	FEB	NOV	MAR	DEC	APR	JAN	MAY	FEB	JUN	MAR	JUL	APR	AUG	MAY	SEP	JUN	OCT	JUL	NOV	AUG	DEC	SEP
1	8	1	8	1	6	1	6	1	5	1	8	1	7	1	8	1	8	1	8	1	8	1	7
2	9	2	9	2	7	2	7	2	6	2	9	2	8	2	9	2	9	2	9	2	9	2	8
3	10	3	10	3	8	3	8	3	7	3	10	3	9	3	10	3	10	3	10	3	10	3	9
4	11	4	11	4	9	4	9	4	8	4	11	4	10	4	11	4	11	4	11	4	11	4	10
5	12	5	12	5	10	5	10	5	9	5	12	5	11	5	12	5	12	5	12	5	12	5	11
6	13	6	13	6	11	6	11	6	10	6	13	6	12	6	13	6	13	6	13	6	13	6	12
7	14	7	14	7	12	7	12	7	11	7	14	7	13	7	14	7	14	7	14	7	14	7	13
8	15	8	15	8	13	8	13	8	12	8	15	8	14	8	15	8	15	8	15	8	15	8	14
9	16	9	16	9	14	9	14	9	13	9	16	9	15	9	16	9	16	9	16	9	16	9	15
10	17	10	17	10	15	10	15	10	14	10	17	10	16	10	17	10	17	10	17	10	17	10	16
11	18	11	18	11	16	11	16	11	15	11	18	11	17	11	18	11	18	11	18	11	18	11	17
12	19	12	19	12	17	12	17	12	16	12	19	12	18	12	19	12	19	12	19	12	19	12	18
13	20	13	20	13	18	13	18	13	17	13	20	13	19	13	20	13	20	13	20	13	20	13	19
14	21	14	21	14	19	14	19	14	18	14	21	14	20	14	21	14	21	14	21	14	21	14	20
15	22	15	22	15	20	15	20	15	19	15	22	15	21	15	22	15	22	15	22	15	22	15	21
16	23	16	23	16	21	16	21	16	20	16	23	16	22	16	23	16	23	16	23	16	23	16	22
17	24	17	24	17	22	17	22	17	21	17	24	17	23	17	24	17	24	17	24	17	24	17	23
18	25	18	25	18	23	18	23	18	22	18	25	18	24	18	25	18	25	18	25	18	25	18	24
19	26	19	26	19	24	19	24	19	23	19	26	19	25	19	26	19	26	19	26	19	26	19	25
20	27	20	27	20	25	20	25	20	24	20	27	20	26	20	27	20	27	20	27	20	27	20	26
21	28	21	28	21	26	21	26	21	25	21	28	21	27	21	28	21	28	21	28	21	28	21	27
22	29	22	29	22	27	22	27	22	26	22	29	22	28	22	29	22	29	22	29	22	29	22	28
23	30	23	30	23	28	23	28	23	27	23	30	23	29	23	30	23	30	23	30	23	30	23	29
24	31	24	1	24	29	24	29	24	28	24	31	24	30	24	31	24	1	24	31	24	31	24	30
25	1	25	2	25	30	25	30	25	1	25	1	25	1	25	1	25	2	25	1	25	1	25	1
26	2	26	3	26	31	26	31	26	2	26	2	26	2	26	2	26	3	26	2	26	2	26	2
27	3	27	4	27	1	27	1	27	3	27	3	27	3	27	3	27	4	27	3	27	3	27	3
28	4	28	5	28	2	28	2	28	4	28	4	28	4	28	4	28	5	28	4	28	4	28	4
29	5			29	3	29	3	29	5	29	5	29	5	29	5	29	6	29	5	29	5	29	5
30	6			30	4	30	4	30	6	30	6	30	6	30	6	30	7	30	6	30	6	30	6
31	7			31	5			31	7			31	7	31	7					31	7	31	7

CHOOSING PROFESSIONAL HELP

It is not easy to decide on whom you wish to help you through your pregnancy and the birth, and you should examine your options carefully before making up your mind. These will vary, depending not just on your finances and your health care plan but on where you live. If you are in a health maintenance organization (HMO), your options may be limited.

Many women, especially those in small towns or rural areas, prefer to stay under the care of their family doctor during pregnancy, because they are familiar and comfortable with him or her. Some general practitioners prefer to refer you to an obstetrician, and, of course, you have the option of choosing an obstetrician – an obstetrician is a doctor who specializes in the care of women during pregnancy and delivery.

Another alternative is to use a midwife. Midwives specialize in the care of mothers and babies during pregnancy, birth and after the delivery. They are completely capable of delivering a baby on their own. (This option may only be available to those living in larger cities.)

Some midwives have independent, private practices and you can arrange for them to look after you for the whole duration of your pregnancy. Others work in partnership with obstetricians. Sometimes, they will come to your home when labor starts, and stay with you through the whole birth. They will only take you to the hospital if it becomes necessary or if it has been arranged previously.

Before you make any decision, it is important that you fully understand what the options involve and that you are completely happy with what is being proposed. You should discuss your concerns and expectations about the birth in detail with your doctor. Don't be intimidated or afraid to ask questions, and remember that the choice is entirely yours. If, for example, your doctor refuses – as some do – to take responsibility for the care of women who want home births, and you would like one, you should change your doctor.

There are a number of different ways in which your care during pregnancy and birth can be managed, and the choice is yours – talk the options over with your family doctor.

YOUR FIRST CONSULTATION

If you haven't consulted your doctor before deciding to become pregnant, you will be able to discuss how you would like your pregnancy to be managed at your first visit – if you see your doctor as soon as you have found that you are pregnant you are likely to be about six to eight weeks into the pregnancy. It will be a long visit, because you will also be asked about your age, past and present health status, whether you have had any operations, certain illnesses or previous pregnancies, or stillbirths or miscarriages. Some medical conditions, such as hypertension, diabetes, cardiac disease, hormonal problems and weight-related problems, require special attention. You will also be asked about your partner's medical history and that of both of your families, in order to rule out the possibility of inherited conditions that may require genetic counseling (see page 51).

Next, your doctor will conduct a physical examination. Your weight will be measured to serve as the baseline as your baby develops; and your height will be checked so that the doctor can estimate the size of your pelvis – just because you are short and slight it does not mean that you are a candidate for cesarean section (see pages 86–87): in fact, shoe size is a more reliable guide to pelvic capacity. Your blood pressure will be taken, and a blood sample taken to test for the following:

◆ blood type;
◆ Rh factor (positive or negative);
◆ anemia;
◆ sensitivity to rubella (German measles);
◆ syphilis;
◆ hepatitis B;
◆ HIV or AIDS (this is not routine, and is only tested, with your permission, in certain cases).

A urine test will be done to test for abnormalities such as sugar or protein in your urine – a little sugar may show from time to time, but if it shows up often you will be checked for diabetes. Protein may appear in your urine either as a result of a urinary infection or as an indication of kidney problems or high blood pressure.

An internal examination may be conducted to confirm the pregnancy by feeling the cervix and assessing the size of your uterus, though some doctors may take an ultrasound scan instead.

A record will be kept of your weight gain throughout your pregnancy.

SUBSEQUENT VISITS

Depending on the system of care that you
have chosen, you will next see your doctor
or midwife every month or second month up
to 28 weeks, then monthly or every two weeks
up to 36 weeks, then every two weeks or weekly
up to 40 weeks (if you carry past your due
date you will be seen every week). An
internal examination may be performed
between 16 and 18 weeks, but otherwise
the visits will be fairly short: your weight,
urine and blood pressure will be
monitored; your baby's heartbeat will be
checked; and your abdomen will be felt
to check the height of the fundus (the top
of the womb) to confirm how the baby
is growing.

36-40 weeks
32 weeks
28 weeks
24 weeks
20 weeks
18 weeks
16 weeks
16 weeks
12 weeks

*The doctor or midwife can check on the baby's growth by feeling
how high the top of the womb is – by the end of the ninth month it
is just below the diaphragm.*

*Gentle aromatherapy massage
from a reputable practitioner is
very relaxing and may help
to relieve tension-related
health problems.*

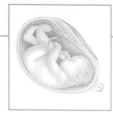

CHAPTER 2

PREGNANCY

Month-by-Month

Pregnancy is divided into three 'trimesters', each about three months long. Many mothers talk about their pregnancy in terms of four-week months, but the medical convention is to refer to the number of weeks of pregnancy, based on the date when your last menstrual period started. A 'standard' pregnancy is considered to last for 40 weeks from this date – rather more than nine months – though anything from 37 to 42 weeks is considered to be normal. In this chapter you will find out what is happening to you and your baby each month, but view the information as a guide, rather than a strict timetable, because every pregnancy is unique. Following medical terminology, 'month 1' starts on the first day of your last period, but remember that conception is likely to be around two weeks later than this.

THE FIRST TRIMESTER

THE BABY'S EXPERIENCE

Month 1: Up to 2 weeks after conception
Once fertilized, the egg continues to move through the fallopian tube and reaches the womb after three to four days. During this time it divides first into two cells, then into four cells, then into eight and so on, in a fantastic explosion of life. Around the outside of this cluster lies a single layer of cells called the trophoblast, which will

eventually form the placenta and the chorion (the outer membrane of the placenta). As part of the process of ovulation, the endometrium (the lining of the womb) has thickened and become enriched with blood in preparation for an embryo, and on around the sixth or seventh day after conception the trophoblast begins to burrow in to it, to link up with the mother's blood supply. This process, called 'implantation', is complete by the tenth day after conception, and the embryo is completely buried inside the endometrium, with the trophoblast starting to form the placenta and triggering the release of the hormones that maintain pregnancy.

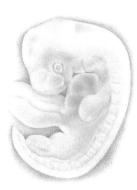

Early in month two the three main systems of the body are formed, and the embryo continues to grow.

Month 2: Weeks 3 to 6 after conception

Now that they are receiving nourishment from the mother, the cells of the embryo, which are still dividing and multiplying, start to differentiate into specialized types of tissue. These form the building blocks of the three major systems of the body: the nervous system, the digestive system and the circulation. By the end of the fourth week after conception the heart is beating (it can be detected by ultrasound) and blood vessels are being formed, though the embryo does not yet produce blood. The neural tube has been laid down, too – this will form the baby's brain and spinal cord; and the rudiments of the digestive system have appeared. The limb buds can be seen and the embryo is now prawn-shaped, with a collection of blood vessels that will form the umbilical cord connecting it to the mother's circulation.

The main systems of the body are now in place and the embryo continues to grow. Lung buds develop, the ears and eyes are developing (but not the eyelids, until the eighth week), the beginnings of hands can be seen, the genito-urinary system is developing (though superficially it is the same in both boy and girl babies) and the liver is starting to produce the embryo's own blood.

During month two the embryo is taking on a shape that is recognizably human, though in the fifth week it is still only about two-fifths of an inch (10mm) long.

Month 3: Weeks 7 to 10 after conception

During the third month the embryo grows quickly – though it is known as a 'fetus' from the eighth week, since it is recognizably human by then – to become around three inches (7.5cm) long. It is already making movements, though the mother cannot feel them, the external genitalia are starting to differentiate and the endocrine glands are beginning to produce hormones. From now on the organs, muscles, limbs and bones will continue to mature and the fetus will grow and gain weight.

By the end of the first trimester the fetus is fully formed. All the organs and body systems are laid down and will grow and mature in the months ahead.

What to do in the first trimester

♦ Organize your first prenatal visit.

♦ Avoid potentially harmful substances such as alcohol, tobacco, drugs, environmental pollutants and any medication that has not been prescribed by a doctor who knows that you are pregnant. This is because all the baby's organs and systems form during the first trimester, so the fetus is at its most vulnerable.

♦ Consult your doctor if you come down with any virus or other illness.

♦ Think about your diet and eating habits, and eat nutritious food.

♦ Examine your lifestyle and think about starting an exercise program, or modifying your existing one.

♦ Ask about your rights at work and available maternity benefits.

♦ Start taking vitamin supplements and – if your doctor advises it – folic acid supplements.

♦ Make an appointment for a dental checkup.

THE MOTHER'S EXPERIENCE

Months 1 to 3: The first 10 weeks after conception

The implantation of the embryo in the lining of your womb triggers the release of the hormones estrogen and progesterone in large quantities, and these affect not only the womb and the development of the placenta but the rest of your body, too. As a result, your periods will stop (though a very few women experience a slight 'show' of blood on the first occasion) and your breasts may start to become enlarged and tender, with the veins becoming more pronounced. A combination of the effect of the hormones and the pressure of your growing womb on your bladder may make you urinate more often, and it is quite common to feel nauseous. Tiredness is common during this trimester, as well – this is because progesterone acts as a sedative.

It is normal to feel somewhat emotional during the first three months, and to experience rapid mood swings, irritability and feelings of ambivalence, even when the pregnancy has been planned. Hormonal changes and the unfamiliar and uncomfortable feelings of early pregnancy are mainly responsible for this, but things settle down in the next trimester, when hormone levels even out and you become more accustomed to your pregnancy.

During the third month (weeks 7 to 10 after conception) you will start to gain weight, your waistline will begin to disappear and your pregnancy may just be starting to show.

In the first trimester of pregnancy your breasts will start to enlarge and your waistline begin to thicken.

THE SECOND TRIMESTER

THE BABY'S EXPERIENCE

Month 4: Weeks 11 to 14 after conception

The intestines are now concealed inside the abdomen, the kidneys are functioning and urine is being produced – it accumulates in the amniotic sac surrounding the baby. The fetus is becoming more and more active.

Month 5: Weeks 15 to 18 after conception

The fetus is very active now and has periods of sleep and wakefulness. It kicks, turns from side to side and sometimes head over heels – you will be able to feel movements from around the 16th week after conception (sometimes a little later if you are a first-time mother). The face is far more human, and hair, eyebrows and eyelashes are beginning to grow; the eyelids are shut. The skin is wrinkled and translucent and covered in fine, soft hair called lanugo.

Month 6: Weeks 19 to 22 after conception

The fetus continues to grow at an astonishing rate, but its organs are still developing. However, sounds can now be heard – especially high frequency ones – and the skin is sensitive to any touch felt through the mother's abdomen. Deposits of fat are building up beneath the skin, making the body start to appear plumper.

At four months (above) the heartbeat is strong and fast. By six months (below) the fetus is much more active and the face looks much more human. Hair, including eyebrows and eyelashes, is now growing and the body is covered in fine hair called lanugo. The skin now looks more reddish.

What to do in the second trimester

- If you have not already done so, enroll in specialized prenatal exercise classes.
- Begin to think about how you want to feed your baby, and what preparations to make.
- Make sure that you do not overdo things – many mothers-to-be find that this is the time when they want to make changes and adjustments in the home.
- Practice relaxation exercises (see pages 54–56) at regular intervals during the day.

THE MOTHER'S EXPERIENCE

Months 4 to 6: Weeks 11 to 22 after conception

If you have felt nauseous and tired during the early weeks of your pregnancy you will probably start to feel better during this trimester. In the fourth month your abdomen swells as your baby grows, and your pregnancy will probably be becoming evident. The other physical changes to expect now are:

- a darkening of the areas around your nipples (the areolas);
- the development of a dark line (linea nigra) on the abdomen, extending from the navel to the pubic hair;
- the appearance of small, dark patches of pigmentation on your face, which are often made worse by exposure to the sun – the phenomenon is known as 'chloasma', and is often referred to as the 'mask of pregnancy';
- an increasing awareness of uterine contractions, known as 'Braxton Hicks' contractions – your womb has been contracting gently since early in your pregnancy, but you do not become aware of it until about 20 weeks.

At the end of the fifth month the fundus (the top of your womb) is at the same level as your navel.

During the sixth month of pregnancy you will gain a lot of weight and will start to look obviously pregnant. You will have felt your baby's movements for the first time, and you may find that you have an increased appetite as your metabolism and energy levels are changing. Many women feel a new surge of energy and vitality at this time and find the second trimester of pregnancy the most enjoyable of the three.

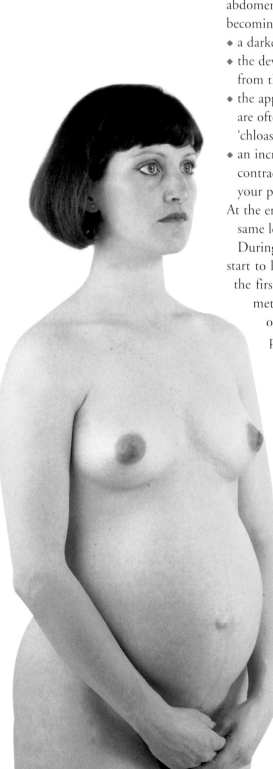

THE THIRD TRIMESTER

THE BABY'S EXPERIENCE

Month 7: Weeks 23 to 26 after conception

The fetus continues to move about vigorously and kicks, stretches and turns somersaults. Sometimes hiccups develop and the mother can feel tiny jerks, but there is no need to be concerned. The fetus is now sucking its thumb and swallowing small amounts of amniotic fluid, and the eyelids are beginning to open. The heartbeat can now be heard through a stethoscope. More fat is being stored under the skin, which is becoming less wrinkled.

You will probably have lots of energy during the second trimester, and many mothers find this the most enjoyable period of their pregnancy.

Month 8: Weeks 27 to 30 after conception

The fetus is still growing, and now measures about 11 inches (280mm) from head to bottom. The white, creamy substance that covers the skin, called the 'vernix caseosa', is now becoming quite thick – it is believed to protect the skin from the amniotic fluid.

Months 9 to 10: Weeks 31 to 38 after conception

This is a time of continued growth, with the baby putting on a considerable amount of weight – mainly muscle tissue and fat. The skeletal system is becoming more rigid, as calcium is laid down, though the skull bones are still flexible and have not yet knitted together. As the due date approaches, the fetus settles into a favorable position for delivery. This usually means that it is lying head down with its knees curled up against its face and its legs tucked tightly against the body. The baby could arrive any time between the 37th and 42nd week of pregnancy.

By seven months the fetus is very active and moves vigorously. It can suck its thumb, swallow amniotic fluid and its eyelids are beginning to open up.

By nine months the fetus has usually settled into a favourable position for birth, with the knees drawn up towards the face and the legs tucked against the body. The baby's head may 'engage', or move down into the mother's pelvis.

THE MOTHER'S EXPERIENCE

Months 7 to 10: Weeks 23 to 38

As you enter the last leg of your pregnancy it is easy to both see and feel the many changes that your body is going through. The baby's rapid growth spurt during month six puts extra pressure on your system, and you may be feeling rather uncomfortable as you enter the third trimester. Some women, though only a few, find that this takes its toll, not only on their body image but their self-esteem. Make sure you get lots of sleep and rest, and ease up on your exercise program if necessary.

Your breasts will become heavier and more pendulous now, as they fill with a watery, sweet fluid called colostrum, which will feed your baby until you produce milk – some women find that it leaks slightly from their breasts during the last month.

You will feel stronger Braxton Hicks contractions in your womb towards the last weeks of your pregnancy, and they may be so intense that you have to stop what you are doing and breathe through them – this is excellent practice for labor. The fundus of the womb comes to lie just beneath the diaphragm, displacing the lungs and making you feel breathless, while your enlarged womb pressures your bladder and makes you need to urinate more often.

The ligaments supporting your joints are now very soft, and you may find that you experience more aches and pains as a result of the extra weight that you are now carrying. Stretchmarks may develop, too, and your hands and feet may swell a little.

As you enter the last weeks of pregnancy (weeks 34 to 38 after conception), you may notice that your baby 'engages', dropping lower into the pelvis (this is also called 'lightening'): breathing will become easier, but you will need to pass urine even more often. Vaginal discharges will increase, but this is quite normal unless they itch, burn or smell offensive.

Your back is likely to ache a lot at this time, so you should pay even more attention to maintaining good posture (see pages 36–37). If you get tired, rest with your feet above the level of your head. Wear comfortable clothes and flat, well-fitting shoes, too, and make sure that your underwear – which should be made of cotton – is large enough for comfort.

What to do in the third trimester

- Start childbirth education classes.
- Start planning your baby's layette.
- Make sure you get enough rest, and don't overdo any exercise.
- Arrange to go on a tour of the hospital in which you are going to have your baby.
- If you have not already done so, start making the necessary arrangements for maternity leave and tell your employer what is happening.
- If you have other children, spend time preparing them for the arrival of the new baby.
- Pack a bag to take to the hospital with you (see pages 67–69)
- Make arrangements for getting to the hospital, and organize a babysitter if you have other children.
- Make sure that all the important telephone numbers – your partner, midwife or doctor, and so on – are at hand in case labor takes you by surprise.

At full term your baby is likely to 'engage', or 'lighten'. This usually makes breathing easier, although pressure on your bladder increases. Make sure you get enough sleep and rest, and enjoy the last weeks before the birth.

CHAPTER 3

A Healthy Pregnancy

Looking After Your Body

Good health is something that no one should take for granted. If you look after yourself properly – by ensuring that, among other things, you receive adequate and appropriate nutrition and exercise – before, during and after pregnancy you will be doing everything you can to help yourself cope with the demands of pregnancy and new motherhood. Remember, too, that you are not only responsible for your own body but also for that of your unborn child.

EATING WELL FOR A HEALTHY PREGNANCY

Your eating habits before and during pregnancy will directly affect not only your own health but also your baby's health and development, and thus it is essential to maintain a healthy, balanced diet. Good nutrition will enhance your immune system, and provide those necessary 'building blocks' from which your baby will grow.

MAJOR DIETARY CONSIDERATIONS DURING PREGNANCY

Meet your increased energy requirements by consuming an extra 300–500 calories a day. Drink at least eight glasses of water a day to meet your body's need for extra fluid. Increase your protein intake by about 30% per day – oily fish are particularly good. Increase your daily calcium intake by 50% early on in pregnancy and start taking folic acid supplements as soon as possible – even before conception if you can. Other vitamin and mineral supplements should only be taken on the advice of your doctor, particularly vitamin A, which may be toxic if taken in excess.

Good eating habits are more important than ever during pregnancy, as the food you eat provides the 'building blocks' from which your baby will grow, and you need all the energy good food will provide.

DIETARY GUIDELINES
- Eat a variety of foods.
- Drink at least a pint of milk a day.
- Eat plenty of high-fiber foods.
- Increase your protein intake, especially of oily fish.
- Eat plenty of foods containing zinc, which is essential for brain development – chops, steak, chicken and nuts for example.
- When preparing food, do so in a way that will preserve as many of the nutrients as possible – grilling, steaming, poaching, stir-frying and microwaving are better than boiling, frying and roasting.
- Eat as many well-washed raw fruits and vegetables as possible. This will increase your fiber and vitamin intake. Vitamin C aids in the absorption of iron, so eat fruits that contain large amounts of this vitamin (these include all citrus fruits).
- Drink at least eight glasses of water a day (over and above your milk intake).
- Have good-quality, nutritious snacks – such as fruit, raw vegetable sticks, whole-grain crackers, milk or fruit juice, plain popcorn, plain yogurt – readily available. Bananas are a great source of instant energy for mornings.

DIETARY DON'TS!
- Don't eat too much fat.
- Don't eat too much sugar.
- Avoid alcohol.
- Avoid smoked foods, since these contain nitrates, which can interfere with the blood's ability to absorb oxygen.
- Avoid caffeine and tannin (coffee, tea and some soft drinks).
- Infection with listeria or salmonella may be contracted from contaminated food, and may cause miscarriage or infection of the fetus. Avoid ripened soft cheeses, pâté, unpasteurized milk and dishes made with raw egg. Prepacked frozen foods, chicken and other meat should be thoroughly cooked. Raw, meat-based pet food should be handled carefully.
- Be careful that you do not consume excessive quantities of vitamin A (from supplementation, from some drugs which are derivatives of vitamin A, or from eating too much liver).

There is no doubt that the nutritional state of the mother has a profound effect on the health and well-being of the fetus and the newborn baby, which will extend into childhood and beyond. Pregnancy is an excellent time to reexamine your eating habits and to form better and healthier guidelines for yourself and your new family.

Keep plenty of fresh and healthy snacks such as fruit salad and muffins available for those moments of the day when hunger strikes. Fresh fruit can be juiced for a refreshing 'pick-me-up' full of vitamins and energy.

Folic acid

Folic acid is a B-group vitamin particularly important for the cells and for cell division. As the rate of cell division in the baby occurs most rapidly during the first three months of pregnancy, while the most important organs are being formed, it is vital to take folic acid at this time. The intake of folic acid both before conception and during pregnancy significantly reduces the risk of neural tube defects such as defects of the spine and spine marrow (spina bifida). If you are planning to become pregnant in the near future, start taking folic acid (folate) supplements (400 mcg daily) and continue to take the supplements throughout early pregnancy.

Dairy and dairy alternatives

This group provides necessary nutrients including calcium, magnesium, complete proteins, fats and vitamins D, B2, B6 and B12. Sources such as cow's or goat's milk, yogurt and cheese are suitable. For people who do not like or cannot tolerate milk products, suitable non-animal alternatives include soy milk, soy bean products such as tofu, and tahini (sesame seed paste).
Portions per day: 2–3.

Bread and cereals

In addition to carbohydrates this important food group provides protein, vitamins B complex and E, iron and traces of other minerals, as well as fiber. Some of the foods which fall into this category are whole-wheat bread and rolls, oatmeal, whole-grain cereals, whole-wheat pasta, brown rice, pearled barley and unrefined corn meal.
Portions per day: 4, or 6 if breastfeeding.

Fats

Fats are an essential component of a balanced diet and are a vital source of energy.
They also store the fat-soluble vitamins A, D, E and K. The best sources of fats
during pregnancy are dairy products, nuts and seeds, eggs, vegetable oils, mayon-
naise and salad dressings. Animal fats and 'junk' foods are best avoided.
Portions per day: 3.

Meat, fish and eggs

In addition to protein, this food group also contains other vital nutrients
such as vitamins A and B complex, iron, phosphorus, calcium and
some other minerals. While many people think of red meat as the
main source of protein, there are many other sources, including
fish, eggs, poultry, legumes, nuts and seeds, and even milk.
Soy beans are an excellent source of non-animal proteins.
Portions per day: 2–3.

Fruits and vegetables

This food group is high in nutrients, low
in calories, and adds color and variety
to meals. Fruits and vegetables provide
vitamins, especially vitamins A, E, C
and K, fiber (which is essential to
help the body get rid of its waste),
minerals and carbohydrates
from natural sugars.
Portions per day:
4 or more if
breastfeeding.

Fiber: 'nature's broom'

Fiber is found in raw fresh fruits
and vegetables and also in a more
concentrated form in cereals such
as coarse bran and whole grains.
Fiber absorbs moisture and adds
bulk to food materials as they
pass through the intestinal tract,
helping to move waste products
quickly through the digestive
system. Adequate intake of fiber
during pregnancy will often ward
off common complaints such as
constipation and hemorrhoids. To
benefit from all types of fiber it is
important to eat a wide variety
of foods and to drink enough
water – this is vital for fiber
to work efficiently.

This 'food pyramid' shows how the different food
groups should be balanced for a healthy diet.

Being underweight can cause as many concerns and problems as being overweight – you should not diet for weight loss during pregnancy. The point of dietary planning during pregnancy is to have a good, nutritious diet so that a healthy mother can give birth to a healthy baby.

WEIGHT GAIN IN PREGNANCY

The general feeling is that, provided she begins her pregnancy at or near her ideal weight, a woman should gain 24–30 lb (11–14 kg) during the pregnancy, based on a prepregnancy weight of 121–165 lb (55–75 kg).

It is important to remember that the rate of weight gain during pregnancy is not uniform: most women put on more weight between the 17th and 20th weeks of pregnancy than at any other period.

The pattern of weight gain is as important as the rate of weight gain. In the first trimester there should be a small weight gain of around 1.5–3 lb (0.7–1.4 kg). During the second and third trimesters a weight gain of 12–16 oz (350–450 g) per week is acceptable.

The weight of pregnancy is made up of the baby, the placenta, the enlarged uterus, stored nutrients and milk glands, as well as the extra blood volume and cellular fluid (see below).

breasts	2 lb (0.9 kg)
baby	7 lb (3.2 kg)
placenta	1.3 lb (0.6 kg)
uterus	3.3 lb (1.5 kg)
blood	3 lb (1.4 kg)
stores	6 lb (2.7 kg)
additional fluid	3.3 lb (1.5 kg)
TOTAL	**25.9 lb (11.8 kg)**

The average weight gain recommended during pregnancy is 24–30 lb (11–14 kg); the extra weight is distributed as illustrated throughout your body.

RISKS IN PREGNANCY

Smoking. Problems associated with smoking include menstrual disorders, infertility, miscarriage, ectopic pregnancy, placental irregularities such as placenta previa and placenta abruptio, low infant birth weight, and sudden infant death after birth. Every attempt should be made to stop smoking or, at least, to cut down.

Alcohol. Alcohol abuse in pregnancy is a major cause of mental retardation of the child. Other problems include growth retardation, low birth weight, central nervous system abnormalities, intrauterine death, miscarriage and developmental delays once the infant is born. Limit alcohol consumption before conception, since it may damage the sperm or ova, and avoid alcohol altogether if you suspect or know you are pregnant.

Drugs. Many drugs (including usually safe ones taken for common ailments such as headaches) can cross the placenta to the fetus and can cause abnormalities, especially in the early part of pregnancy. Educate yourself before conception about the risks of any medication or drugs you are using and, if necessary, seek advice. Do not, however, discontinue any prescribed medication without consulting your doctor – the health risk posed by the untreated condition may outweigh the risk of damage to the fetus. All so-called 'recreational drugs' should be avoided.

Caffeine. Caffeine is readily absorbed by the fetal bloodstream so it is wise to limit or stop your caffeine consumption both before conception and during pregnancy. It is found in tea, coffee, some carbonated drinks, and many headache, flu and cold remedies. Check the labels on all medicines, foods and soft drinks for caffeine.

PRENATAL EXERCISE

Appropriate exercise in pregnancy forms your physical preparation for labor, birth and motherhood. Labor, as the name suggests, is hard work and, even if you have a cesarean delivery, knowing that your body is fit and has the strength and stamina to see you through the pregnancy, the birth and early motherhood will give you extra confidence.

IS IT SAFE TO EXERCISE?

It is safe to continue your usual exercise routine during a normal, uncomplicated pregnancy. Even if you haven't exercised before you can safely begin an exercise program during pregnancy and can become fit provided that you take regular, moderate and safe exercise. Permission from your doctor or midwife and the supervision of a qualified health professional are essential.

Subject to medical approval, you can begin exercising right away. Exercise is good for the developing baby: it oxygenates and stimulates the blood flow, it produces a surge of adrenalin, it releases endorphins which increase relaxation and contentment, and the regular motion involved in exercise is soothing for the baby. Don't overdo it, however. Even the fittest women experience fatigue and lethargy in the early months of pregnancy, so slow down and keep exercise to a minimum.

Note that exercising during pregnancy does not necessarily mean that your labor will be easy, short and without complications, but whatever you experience during labor, your body and mind will cope better if you are fit and strong.

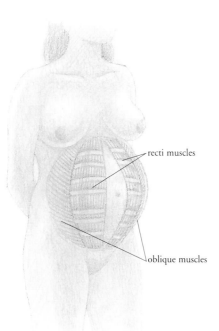

recti muscles

oblique muscles

During mid- to late pregnancy the recti muscles of the abdomen will start to separate. This is called divarication of the recti muscles.

TYPES OF EXERCISE

Suitable types of exercise include brisk walking (not jogging), cycling, low-impact aerobics (your program must be modified to allow for pregnancy), dancing and swimming. Yoga is excellent for stretching and toning muscles, increasing flexibility, mental relaxation and for learning controlled breathing techniques. Calisthenics must be modified to suit your flexibility and stage of pregnancy. Circuit training should be continued only under the supervision of a qualified health professional. If you played regularly before your pregnancy, it is safe to continue with sports such as tennis during the first trimester.

ABDOMINAL MUSCLES

It is important to exercise your abdominal muscles during pregnancy as these muscles must make many adaptations, and strong abdominals assist in maintaining good posture. You will also use these muscles in the expulsive stage of labor when you push your baby out.

You should not perform any inappropriate abdominal exercises during your pregnancy as they may place strain on an already stretched set of muscles. Weight-bearing, crunch-type sit-ups are not recommended. Your abdominals have a built-in safety mechanism – from about 20 weeks (five months of pregnancy) the recti muscles, which run vertically from the breastbone straight down to the pelvis, will start to separate slightly over the apex of the uterus. This painless separation is called divarication or diastasis of the recti muscles. Most women notice the change when lying in the bath or getting out of bed. The soft tissues beneath the recti bulge gently just above and just below the mother's navel. Strenuous abdominal exercise will cause further separation and should not be encouraged. This condition will usually right itself shortly after the birth.

Checking for divarication (separation)

Lie on your back with knees bent and feet flat on the floor. Place the fingers of one hand just above your navel. Place the other hand behind your head and slowly raise your head off the floor, exhaling as you do so and tightening your abdominal wall. In this position use your fingers to feel gently for the edge of the muscles or the gap between them. Check how many fingers will fit in the gap. One or two fingers is normal, but three to four fingers mean that you should modify your program of abdominal exercises.

When you check for divarication of the recti muscles make sure that you support your head with one hand while you feel for the gap in the abdominal wall with the other.

Abdominal exercises
Pelvic tilt
This basic exercise will help you develop and maintain abdominal strength, and take pressure off the lower back.

◆ Lie on your back with your knees bent, feet hip-width apart, not too close to the buttocks and not too far away.

◆ Keeping your back flat on the ground, bring the front of your pelvis towards your rib cage as you tighten the abdominal muscles in towards the navel. Do not hold your breath, but exhale as you do this. Hold for the count of five.

◆ To release, slowly relax your abdominal muscles and release the pelvis while breathing in.

◆ If you are not comfortable doing this on your back, especially in the advanced stages of pregnancy, this exercise can be performed in the all-fours position (also an extremely comfortable position for labor, especially if you are experiencing pain in your lower back), or standing up – with or without a wall for support.

When standing up *to do a pelvic tilt, use your abdominal muscles to press your back into the wall.*

Kneel on a small mat *or pillow with your arms at your sides. Focus on your abdominal muscles and gently tighten them by pulling them in towards your navel, at the same time squeezing your buttocks together. You may wish to link your fingers, turning your wrists outwards, and push your arms forward to shoulder height as you squeeze your abdominals and buttocks, but this is optional.*

Lie on your side *with your knees slightly bent towards your chin, 'stack' your pelvic bones, and support your head with your lower hand. Focusing on your adominal muscles, draw your navel in towards your spine to 'hug' your baby as the muscles tighten, exhaling as you do so. Release while inhaling, and then repeat slowly.*

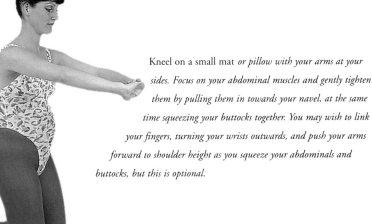

Kneel on all fours *with your neck extending naturally forward from the top of your spine (that is, keep the back of your head level with your spine). Your back should be flat and not dropped and hollow. Draw your abdominal muscles up and in towards your spine, exhaling as you do so. Release gently and inhale.*

Modified aerobic exercise *during pregnancy is considered to be safe, and will enhance your fitness. Using training aids such as light, hand-held weights and a 'step' box will add creativity to your routine. However, incorporate these tools into your exercise program only under the guidance of an informed fitness instructor.*

IMPROVING YOUR STRENGTH AND FITNESS

An inexpensive child's ball *is a great aid for exercising at home. To strengthen your pectoral muscles, place the ball between your palms keeping your elbows at shoulder height, and squeeze. For a variation, tilt gently to one side and then to the other as you squeeze the ball; this will also exercise the oblique abdominal muscles.*

Sitting in a supported squat *will increase the flexibility of your groin and inner thigh area, which is a decided advantage in labor. Use a pile of three or four telephone books or a low stool as a support. Pelvic floor (Kegel) exercises can be done very effectively in this position — see page 36.*

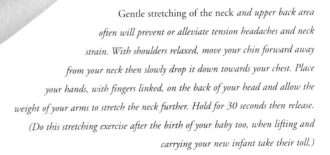

This exercise, *commonly known as the 'Charley Horse', helps to prevent those nasty cramps in your calf. Lean your forearms against a wall. Place your left leg forward with the knee slightly bent and toes against the wall, and extend your right leg back, keeping your foot flat against the floor with the heel down. Hold this position for 30 seconds, and then change sides.*

Gentle stretching of the neck *and upper back area often will prevent or alleviate tension headaches and neck strain. With shoulders relaxed, move your chin forward away from your neck then slowly drop it down towards your chest. Place your hands, with fingers linked, on the back of your head and allow the weight of your arms to stretch the neck further. Hold for 30 seconds then release. (Do this stretching exercise after the birth of your baby too, when lifting and carrying your new infant take their toll.)*

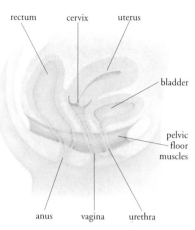

rectum   cervix   uterus

bladder

pelvic
floor
muscles

anus   vagina   urethra

Pelvic floor *muscles*

PELVIC FLOOR MUSCLES

The pelvic floor is a group of muscles that form a sling spanning the area from the pubic bone in the front to the coccyx (base of the spine) at the back. The sheet-like muscular structure, which is affected by the hormones of pregnancy, supports the bladder, bowel and uterus and helps to control the functions of these organs, acting quickly when you cough, laugh or sneeze. Well-toned pelvic floor muscles also help to increase sexual satisfaction for both partners during intercourse. A strong pelvic floor assists the abdominal muscles, thereby relieving strain on the back muscles and helping you to maintain good posture. Weak pelvic floor muscles also affect urinary continence and your quality of life.

It is important that you find the time to contract these muscles at regular times during the day by doing pelvic floor muscle exercises (see below). Make this a life-long habit. As these muscles tire fairly quickly, don't do too many contractions at once – rather do 10–20 contractions whenever you think about it during the day.

Pelvic floor exercise

Locate the pelvic muscles when on the toilet by stopping your flow of urine midstream. Release, then once the bladder is empty tighten up again, hold for a few seconds and release. This is not to be done routinely as it could cause urinary retention. Once you have located your muscles, do the following pelvic floor exercise. Get into a comfortable position – lie on your side, sit forward on a chair, tailor-sit (sitting upright on the floor with knees bent and the soles of the feet drawn together) or squat. Without tightening your buttocks, abdominal muscles or inner thighs, pull up the muscles in your vagina and imagine you are squeezing a tampon.

Slow, strong, controlled contractions are preferable to quick, up-and-down lifts. Imagining that you are lifting the pelvic floor in stages and holding each stage for two seconds is a slightly more creative way of doing a potentially boring exercise (often referred to as the elevator exercise). No matter how boring, do not become lazy – a well-toned pelvic floor will stretch like a piece of new elastic, and this will be very helpful during second-stage labor when you push your baby out.

WHEN SHOULD YOU STOP EXERCISING?

You can exercise until the day you deliver, but if you feel tired and sore you may wish to stop sooner. It is important to listen to and take your cue from your body. Your doctor or midwife may advise you to stop exercising – always heed this advice.

POSTURAL AWARENESS

Good posture – never more important than during pregnancy – means less fatigue and irritability, and fewer aches and pains. Good posture also helps to prevent the chronic back pain which is so common during pregnancy. Pregnancy tends to highlight your postural flaws, and it will take conscious effort to change bad habits. Exercise will help you to adjust your posture and to maintain alignment and balance.

Check your posture

- Stand sideways in front of a full-length mirror. Place your feet hip-width apart, with your weight forward towards the balls of the feet. The center of your body should be directly above the arches of your feet.
- Don't stiffen or lock your knees – this will throw your weight backward and increase the curve in your lower back. Ensure that your knees are relaxed and directly above the arches of your feet.
- Tilt the front of your pelvis upward and tuck in your buttocks. This involves all of the abdominal muscles and lengthens the lower back muscles.
- Hold your head up high, and straighten and lengthen your neck, keeping your chin parallel to the floor. The back of your head should be vertically in line with your upper back.
- Drop your shoulders so that they are relaxed and not pulled up towards the ears.

Points to remember

- Avoid standing for long periods and avoid being in one position for too long.
- Do not fill your handbag to capacity, and don't carry heavy backpacks.
- When carrying packages, learn to divide the load between both hands and balance the weight equally, or ask for help.

Poor posture *strains your back.*

Good posture *eases backache.*

CORRECT LIFTING

Bend your knees *when lifting things.*

Correct lifting requires that you use your legs to assist the back and abdominal muscles. Use the following guidelines to lift objects (heavy or light) without straining your back:

- Stand with your feet hip-width apart.
- Face the direction that you are going to move off in. (If you lift and twist at the same time you will put great pressure on the spine.)
- Move down towards the object by bending your knees and 'sinking' towards it, allowing one knee to touch the floor and keeping the other up off the ground.

Do not *keep your legs straight.*

◆ Never bend forward from the hips with straight legs! Use the large muscles of the legs to do the bending and not the thin, strap-like muscles of the back.

◆ Bring the object close to your body. Lift it slowly, pushing up with the large muscles of the legs and keeping your back upright. Your center of gravity should remain stable, with your weight equally distributed between both legs.

◆ As you rise, keep your chin tucked in – do not thrust it forward to lead the way. Brace your abdominal and back muscles, but let the large thigh muscles do most of the work.

When rising from a lying position, turn onto your side and use your arms, then your legs, to push yourself up (above). Do not pull yourself up with your abdominal muscles (right), as this causes strain.

MAKING LOVE

Many couples worry unnecessarily about the safety of sex during pregnancy. There is no reason for you to discontinue sexual intercourse during a normal pregnancy. You will not endanger the fetus, as the penis cannot penetrate beyond the vagina – the mucous plug and the muscles of the cervix seal off the uterus completely.

Generally, you may find that your libido fluctuates throughout your pregnancy. As pregnancy progresses you may need to experiment and explore different positions. It is important to communicate openly with your partner, and to be sensitive to each other's needs so that you are fully aware of what is and is not comfortable for each other.

If you have previously had a miscarriage or problems with your cervix, consult your doctor. An incompetent cervix may require stitching as a precaution against miscarriage. Your doctor may advise you to avoid intercourse in the early months of pregnancy if you have had problems in the past or suffered heavy bleeding during a previous pregnancy.

Orgasm or even intercourse itself can cause the uterus to contract and the abdomen to become hard as the hormone oxytocin is released into your system. There is no need for alarm – if it feels uncomfortable, lie quietly and let it pass.

Sexual intercourse is also a pleasurable way of starting labor, as the prostaglandins in semen stimulate the uterus, but only if the cervix is ripe and ready. Once the bag of waters is broken, however, intercourse is not advisable.

HEALTH ISSUES

COMMON COMPLAINTS IN PREGNANCY

For many women pregnancy is a time when their bodies 'glow and grow' without any problems or concerns at all. However, each pregnancy is different, and it is not uncommon to experience some of the following common but minor complaints and discomforts. Try the accompanying helpful hints and suggestions to ease any problems that might develop.

Backache. The hormones produced during pregnancy have the effect of making body tissues become softer and joints become lax. Increased abdominal strain impacts on the muscles of the back, which end up bearing the full load of pregnancy; bad posture will exacerbate any backache.
Helpful hints. Good posture is vital (see pages 36–37). Prenatal exercise classes will help build muscle strength and suppleness, which will prevent or alleviate your discomfort. Learn how to lift things correctly (see pages 37–38). Ask your partner to massage your back. Avoid high-heeled shoes, and do pelvic tilt exercises. If your backache is extremely painful, consult a physical therapist for advice on specific exercises that can help relieve the problem.

Bladder discomfort. During the first and third trimesters of pregnancy you will feel the need to urinate more often. Your body produces more urine and, as the weight of the uterus adds pressure to your bladder, you will feel uncomfortable. You may also experience 'leaking' from the bladder when you cough, laugh, or sneeze; this is due to added strain on the muscles of the pelvic floor.
Helpful hints. Exercise your pelvic floor muscles daily by doing pelvic floor exercises (see page 36). Empty your bladder as soon as you feel your body's cues, and do not limit your fluid intake. You are more susceptible to bladder infections during pregnancy, so if you experience any burning when you pass urine contact your doctor immediately.

Bleeding gums. There is greater blood flow to the gums during pregnancy, increasing the likelihood of bleeding gums.

Helpful hints. Don't be alarmed. Use a softer toothbrush than usual, floss regularly and use mouthwash frequently. Eat fruits that are high in vitamin C. Make sure that you have a check-up with your dentist during your pregnancy.

Carpal tunnel syndrome. A few women experience some degree of tingling, pain and weakness in one of their hands, sometimes feeling numbness as high up as the forearm. This sensation of 'pins and needles' is caused by pressure from fluid retention on one of the nerves that passes in front of the wrist.

Helpful hints. Rotate your wrist gently to increase blood circulation, avoid carrying heavy packages and avoid extreme flexing of the wrist. Try to keep your hand raised above the elbow. Try not to lie on the affected side while sleeping. If the pain is unbearable, consult your doctor as you may need a course of low-dosage diuretics, or, rarely, a minor operation under local anesthetic.

Constipation. The pregnancy hormone progesterone slows down the intestinal tract, increasing digestion time and increasing the uptake of water. Bad or irregular eating habits, insufficient fiber and water in your diet, and lack of exercise will make any constipation worse.

Helpful hints. Examine your diet and make the necessary adjustments. Avoid fatty foods and eat more prunes, figs and high-fiber foods. Drink plenty of water. Go to the toilet as soon as you feel the urge (put your feet up on a footstool to minimize straining). Exercise – even a brisk walk – and relaxation will also help. Do not take laxatives.

Cramps. These are very common, especially in the calves and feet towards the latter part of pregnancy. Experts believe that cramps are a result of an imbalance of the minerals calcium and phosphorus, and a lack of sodium.

Helpful hints. Ensure that you have enough calcium in your diet. Do exercises that stimulate the circulation of blood to the muscles of the leg. Keep them warm, and avoid pointing the toes during exercises. Gentle massage towards the heart is very soothing after a cramp attack.

Flexing your foot towards your knee will help to relieve leg cramps. As your stomach gets larger, use a towel to help you stretch the muscles at the back of the legs.

Dizziness. Sometimes when you stand up quickly you may feel a little strange or 'spaced out' for a short time as your body adjusts to your new position.

Helpful hints. Remember to stand up slowly, and have your blood pressure checked. Be sure that your diet is adequate and do not leave long periods between meals; keep some healthy snacks close at hand in case you get hungry.

Heartburn. The strong, burning pain of heartburn, which can be felt in the chest close to the heart, must be one of the most common complaints of pregnancy. The pregnancy hormones soften and relax the stomach valve, allowing stomach acid to pass into the esophagus. Certain positions and pressure from the abdominal organs may exacerbate this problem.

Helpful hints. Eat smaller meals more frequently, but not before going to bed. Drink milk to neutralize stomach acid. Avoid spicy or acidic foods. Eat slowly and chew your food well. Check with your pharmacist before taking an antacid.

Joint pain. During pregnancy the hormone relaxin softens the ligaments of the pelvis in preparation for birth. This may cause pain in the hips, buttocks, pubic area and back, which is exacerbated by poor posture.

Helpful hints. There is no quick fix for this discomfort. Avoid painful positions or movements, and improve your posture. Apply heat and gentle massage to any painful areas. Do not sit or stand for too long.

Morning sickness. Nausea, one of the first signs of pregnancy, is common in the first weeks. While some women only feel nauseous, others actually vomit. Nausea may occur at any time of the day or night, and normally disappears after the third month. It can leave you feeling tired, drained, emotional and unable to cope. While the cause of morning sickness is not fully understood, the good news is that research shows nausea in pregnancy to be associated with good fetal health.

Note: Report persistent vomiting to your doctor.

Helpful hints. To alleviate morning sickness, eat a dry cracker or a piece of toast on waking, and give yourself a little extra time to rise. Avoid tea or coffee and drink herbal teas instead of ordinary tea. Drink plenty of fluid. Eat small meals more frequently and, of course, avoid foods that make you feel worse. Make sure you get lots of fresh air.

Hemorrhoids. These are small swellings in the rectal area which may itch, ache or feel sore during or after a bowel movement, and may even bleed slightly. They, too, are due to hormonal influences which cause the anal veins to soften and enlarge. Constipation will aggravate hemorrhoids.

Helpful hints. Avoid constipation. Do not sit on the toilet for long periods of time, and raise your feet onto a footstool, low box or pile of telephone books during a bowel movement to avoid straining. Cotton wool pads soaked in witch hazel and applied to the painful area will shrink and soothe piles. Remember to do pelvic floor exercises to strengthen your pelvic floor muscles.

Round ligament strain. This is a stitchlike pain commonly felt along the right side of the abdomen. An awkward, sudden movement may initiate this painful spasm.

Helpful hints. As soon as you feel it lie down on the affected side, relax and breathe deeply. Try not to tense up or 'move away' from the pain as this will only make it worse. If you are unable to lie down, deep breathing will help.

Swelling (edema). Fluid retention due to the influence of the pregnancy hormones is very common, and it can cause swelling in the hands, feet and ankles as well as a taut feeling in the skin. It is likely to occur in the last trimester and may be worse in hot weather or at the end of the day. If swelling is accompanied by high blood pressure or protein in the urine it may be a sign of a more serious condition known as preeclampsia (see page 45). Consult your doctor if you are at all worried.

Helpful hints. Avoid standing for long periods. Exercise to improve your circulation. Drink according to your thirst, and do not cut down on your fluid intake. Limit your intake of salt.

Vaginal discharge. It is normal to have a thin mucous discharge that is almost colorless. If, however, this discharge starts to itch, burn or smell offensive you must seek treatment from your doctor.

Helpful hints. Do not use tampons, feminine hygiene sprays, bath oils and so on during pregnancy. Wear cotton underwear.

SPECIAL HEALTH CONCERNS AND COMPLICATIONS

AIDS

This is caused by the human immuno-deficiency virus (HIV). HIV damages the immune system, the body's natural defense, leaving it open to harmful infections which will eventually cause the sufferer to die. HIV is spread via body fluids, such as semen and blood, through sexual contact or transfusions with infected blood, as well as through infected needles used for injections. As the virus is able to cross the placenta before birth, it may spread to the fetus through the mother's blood during pregnancy. HIV is also present in breast milk and can be passed on to the baby in this way even if the mother becomes infected after the delivery. Women who are infected with HIV need special counseling to help them make decisions such as whether to get pregnant, whether to request termination of pregnancy, methods of delivery, and whether to breastfeed.

Diabetes in pregnancy

With good care, a diabetic woman can have a healthy pregnancy and baby. Many of the body's requirements change during pregnancy. Pregnancy hormones have an anti-insulin effect, and increased insulin will be needed. It is a good idea to have your condition assessed before you become pregnant, if possible, so that potential problems specific to diabetes can be avoided. A diabetic woman is more likely to develop urinary tract and vaginal infections, so she will have more prenatal check-ups than usual. The aim of good diabetic care is to control blood sugar meticulously. A pregnant diabetic woman may need to check her blood three or more times a day and may need up to three times her usual daily insulin dose. Her insulin requirements are likely to be adjusted several times during pregnancy but will fall back to normal after the birth. If you are diabetic, it is important to check all aspects of your daily life with your doctor, including your diet and any exercise program.

Gestational diabetes

Today, all pregnant women should be screened for diabetes. If sugar is discovered in the urine of a pregnant woman who is not normally diabetic then gestational diabetes may be suspected. With early diagnosis and good prenatal care most babies born to these mothers are healthy and normal, but there is a risk of prematurity and a larger-than-normal baby. Treatment may only involve making adjustments to diet, or it may be necessary to receive insulin if the blood sugars are not well controlled.

Multiple pregnancy

A multiple pregnancy is one where more than one fetus is present, and is usually confirmed when two or more heartbeats are heard. Multiple pregnancies – usually twins – occur in just over one percent of pregnancies. Signs of multiple pregnancy include a family history of twins, rapid weight gain and uterine growth in excess of the normal rate.

Multiple pregnancy increases the risk of certain problems to both the mother and the babies, and early diagnosis is important. It is routine to have more frequent prenatal visits than usual as well as more ultrasound scans.

The most favorable presentation for the vaginal delivery of twins is when both babies are vertex, or head down (below left). If one twin is vertex and the other breech (below right), your obstetrician may recommend a cesarean delivery.

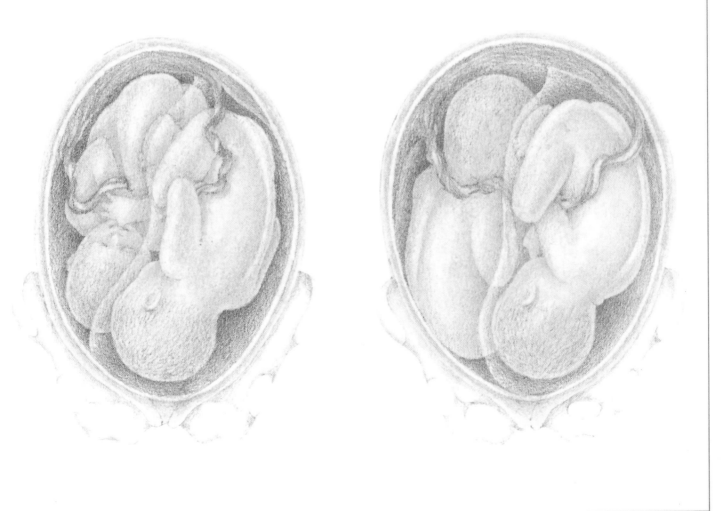

Your delivery options are limited with a multiple pregnancy since, depending upon the position of the babies within the uterus, the birth may be more complicated. There is a greater than usual chance that your babies will be born by cesarean section (see pages 86–90).

Placental problems (see also pages 87 and 99)

Placenta previa. This is a condition where the placenta is implanted either completely or partially over the cervix, thereby obstructing the birth canal. A 'low-lying' placenta seen on ultrasound in early pregancy will often 'move' to a normal position as the uterus grows. A sign of placenta previa is painless vaginal bleeding after the seventh month of pregnancy, with no apparent cause and which may occur during rest or sleep as well as during activity. Your baby is likely to be born by cesarean section, but this decision will only be made close to the due date. The cause of placenta previa is unknown, but it seems to occur more frequently in women who have had several children, and in mature mothers.

Placenta abruptio. This is a very serious condition in which the placenta starts to come away from the wall of the uterus (occurring in only 0.5% of pregnancies). Although it occurs in differing degrees, it may be life-threatening for the fetus as extensive separation of the placenta will deprive the baby of oxygen and cause fetal distress. Placenta abruptio is more likely to occur in the third trimester of pregnancy or during labor, and is more common in women who have had more than one pregnancy or who are malnourished. An emergency cesarean section under a general anesthetic is the most likely method of delivery.

A low-lying placenta (above) may partially cover the cervix, but often moves out of the way as pregnancy progresses. True placenta previa (right), with the placenta covering the cervix completely, is not common.

Preeclampsia (toxemia of pregnancy)

This serious condition is, for some reason, more common in first-time mothers. Those in their teens or women over 30 are at more risk. It usually develops in the second trimester. The signs of preeclampsia include:

◆ high blood pressure;
◆ a sudden and excessive retention of fluid;
◆ increased weight gain;
◆ protein in the urine;
◆ disturbed vision;
◆ dizziness;
◆ severe headaches.

Should you experience any of these symptoms report them to your doctor immediately. If untreated, preeclampsia may progress to eclampsia, which causes convulsions, coma and the death of the baby or mother. Close medical attention is necessary, with the lowering of the blood pressure being the main aim, and bed rest is prescribed. The type of delivery will depend upon the severity of the condition, and may vary from a cesarean section to early induction of labor under close supervision.

Hyperemesis gravidarum

Unlike morning sickness (see page 41), this is severe vomiting that continues throughout the day, causing severe weight loss and dehydration. Always report vomiting to your doctor or midwife, especially if it occurs three or more times in a day. Treatment is usually very effective, and may involve a short stay in the hospital with fluids given into a vein by an intravenous drip to correct your electrolyte imbalance, as well as medication to relieve the vomiting and nausea.

Rh incompatibility

The Rhesus or Rh factor is a substance found on the surface of red blood cells. You are considered to be Rh positive if, like most of the population, you have this substance. When the Rh factor is absent, the blood is classified as Rh negative. It is important to determine the Rh factor of a pregnant woman early on in the pregnancy, through a routine blood test.

If the mother tests Rh negative and the baby is Rh positive, there is a possibility that Rh-positive blood cells from the baby could pass across the placenta into the mother's bloodstream during the pregnancy or at birth. Here they are recognized as foreign, and the mother may produce Rh-positive antibodies to kill these cells. If this is the mother's first pregnancy it is unlikely that

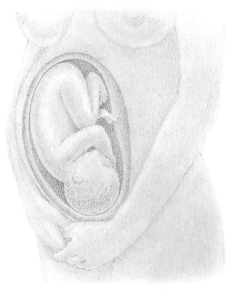

Rh incompatibility occurs when the mother's blood is Rh negative, but her baby's is Rh positive. It is important to do a simple blood test early in pregnancy to establish the mother's Rh factor.

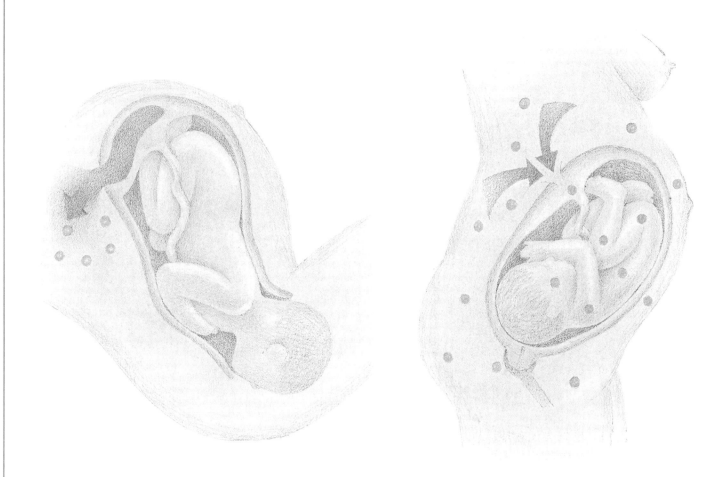

During the pregnancy or at birth, Rh-positive blood cells from the baby may cross the placenta into the mother's bloodstream (above left). Here they are recognized as foreign and the mother may produce Rh antibodies to kill these cells. If she is not treated with a Rh-immune-globulin injection at the end of the pregnancy, she will build up antibodies which may attack a Rh-positive baby in a subsequent pregnancy (above right).

the baby will be affected as she will probably have very few, if any, antibodies. However, if she is not treated at the end of the pregnancy she will build up antibodies and there is then a strong chance that a Rh-positive baby in a subsequent pregnancy could be harmed, resulting in jaundice, anemia, heart failure or brain damage.

To prevent this the Rh-negative mother is given an injection of Rh-immune-globulin (a RhoGam injection) each time she delivers a Rh-positive baby. If a mother is Rh negative with antibodies present, the amount of antibodies in her blood system must be monitored throughout her pregnancy.

Sexually transmitted diseases (STDs)

These are diseases that are spread or transmitted through sexual contact. Sexually transmitted diseases may affect a woman's chance of conceiving and, if present during pregnancy, may infect and harm the fetus.

Chlamydia, gonorrhea and pelvic inflammatory disease (PID). These severe infections start in the vagina and can spread through to the cervix and the entire pelvic area, including the uterus, fallopian tubes and ovaries. Women with these infections often have no symptoms and will only be alerted to the problem when their partner is diagnosed; men will experience a penis that 'drips'. If the fetus is infected with chlamydia or gonorrhea during the birth, eye infections as well as other serious problems can result.

Herpes simplex virus. This virus causes genital herpes. It is transmitted through sexual contact with a person who has an active infection, and causes sores and blisters to develop around the sex organs. If a mother has signs of an active infection close to her delivery date the doctor may consider a cesarean delivery to prevent the baby coming into contact with the virus in the vagina. Infection of the fetus in the birth canal may cause skin infections, blindness, and damage to the nervous system which may result in mental retardation.

Syphilis. Syphilis – now a fairly rare condition – is a dangerous, highly contagious disease which can cause the fetus to be blind and to have problems with the development of the nervous system, skin, bones, liver, lungs and spleen. It is easier to detect in men than in women, who may have a sore inside the vagina where it can pass unnoticed. Diagnosis can be made by a routine prenatal blood test. It is important to treat the mother as soon as possible, and treatment is simple and easy, consisting of penicillin injections at varying intervals.

OTHER WARNING SIGNS IN PREGNANCY

If you experience any of the following symptoms during your pregnancy please contact your doctor immediately, as they could be signs of a more serious underlying problem:

- vaginal bleeding;
- abdominal pain;
- pain between the navel and the rib cage;
- leaking or gushing of fluid from the vagina;
- dizziness or lightheadedness;
- sudden puffiness or swelling of the hands, face and feet;
- severe, persistent headache;
- pain or burning on passing urine;
- disturbance of vision, spots, flashes or blind spots in the field of vision;
- any vaginal discharge, sores and/or itching;
- temperature over 100.5° F (38° C);
- persistent nausea or vomiting;
- noticeable reduction in the baby's movements.

It is important that you make contact with your doctor so as to diagnose problems early on in your pregnancy. Early diagnosis will also help to alleviate any unnecessary anxiety that you may be experiencing. Always follow your instincts and don't be afraid to ask questions, so that you understand what is happening to you, your body and your baby.

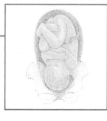

CHAPTER 4

A WINDOW INTO THE WOMB

Tests During Pregnancy

Modern technology allows us a 'window into the womb', enabling us to detect complications or abnormalities at an early stage of pregnancy. This allows for an early diagnosis and, where possible, early treatment. Before you make a decision about whether to have any prenatal tests, examine your reasons for wanting them. Explore your feelings about what steps, if any, you would want to take should any of these tests prove that you are carrying a baby that is not completely normal. Discussion with your partner, family and friends as well as your doctor is essential. It is important to note that the reasons for many birth defects are still unknown. Causes may be genetic, environmental or multifactoral; however, 93% of all babies are born with no problems.

An ultrasound scan provides you with your first opportunity to 'see' your baby: often a thrilling and reassuring experience.

TESTS IN EARLY PREGNANCY

Triple test (Down's screen). This is a blood test taken at 15–16 weeks. Three hormones from the baby and placenta are measured: alpha-fetoprotein, chorionic gonadotrophin and estriol. Abnormal levels of these hormones may indicate an increased risk of your baby having either spina bifida or a chromosome disorder such as Down's syndrome. The test does not determine whether your baby is affected or not; it only gives a risk factor. If this is high, further screening in the form of an ultrasound scan and/or an amniocentesis will be offered to you.

Amniocentesis. This test is conducted at about 16 weeks of pregnancy if any abnormality is suspected. It will be offered to a mother over 35 years old, for whom there is a higher risk of having a baby with Down's syndrome. It will also be offered if the triple test indicates a high risk factor, although if spina bifida is suspected a detailed ultrasound scan may be sufficient for diagnosis. Amniocentesis may also be recommended if the parents' families have a history of Down's syndrome, hemophilia, spina bifida, cystic fibrosis or other genetic conditions. Amniocentesis may be performed later in pregnancy to determine lung maturity, and hence the age of the fetus, or Rh incompatibility. It also reveals the sex of the fetus.

Amniocentesis carries a very small – less than one percent – risk of miscarriage. It is important that you are fully aware of the risks and benefits of this particular test. The procedure for an amniocentesis involves an ultrasound scan to check the position of the baby, the placenta and the umbilical cord, and to guide the needle into the amniotic sac. A local anesthetic is given to numb the skin. A needle is then passed through the abdominal and uterine wall into the amniotic fluid surrounding the baby. A sample of the fluid is drawn off and tested. The test results for spina bifida will be available within a few days, but the results for Down's syndrome may take up to a month.

Chorionic villus sampling. This test can be done from as early as 10–12 weeks of pregnancy. However, it has a higher risk of miscarriage and is unable to detect spina bifida. An ultrasound scan is used to guide a fine tube with a syringe attached to the end of it through the vagina and cervix. Alternatively, a needle may be passed through the abdominal wall. A sample of several of the finger-like projections known as chorionic villi is taken from the chorion, the protective layer around the amniotic sac. These villi are genetically identical to the embryo, and analysis of these cells will provide genetic information about the fetus. The results of this test are available within a few days. Genetic disorders such as hemophilia, muscular dystrophy, cystic fibrosis, Huntington's chorea, Tay-Sachs disease, thalassemia and sickle-cell anemia can be diagnosed with this test.

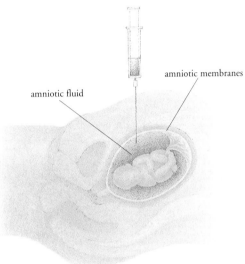

amniotic fluid

amniotic membranes

An amniocentesis can be performed at about 16 weeks of pregnancy to test for fetal abnormalities. A fine needle is passed into the amniotic sac and a sample of amniotic fluid is drawn off for testing.

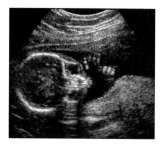

A frontal view shows the head and clenched fists of this 20-week-old baby.

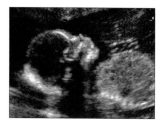

A profile of the same baby shows that by this stage the face is well developed.

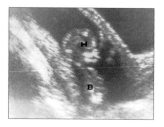

This scan shows the position of the 12-week-old baby in the uterus.

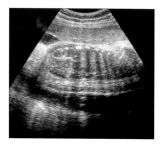

The spine and ribs of this baby are clearly shown in the ultrasound scan.

Cordocentesis. Using ultrasound as a guide, a needle is passed through the abdomen into the umbilical cord to draw off a sample of the baby's blood. The test is used to detect a range of defects such as hemophilia, blood platelet disorders or Rh incompatibility (see pages 45–46), and infections such as toxoplasmosis, rubella or herpes. It is a low risk procedure and can be done at any time from 18 weeks until full term.

TESTS IN LATER PREGNANCY

Fetal movement counts. This involves the mother counting and recording the time of the baby's tenth movement each day. (It is normal for a baby to move at least ten times in 12 hours.) The test assists in the assessment of the well-being of the fetus and is noninvasive, but it is not always very reliable as it involves awareness and commitment from the mother, who may not recognize all the fetal movements. The advantage of this test is that it will usually reassure the mother about the condition of her baby as she realizes how active it is; however, it also has the potential to alarm her if she feels that the baby is not moving as much as it should.

Non-stress test. The mother is attached to an external fetal heart monitor, and the fetal heartbeat as well as fetal movements and rest periods are recorded for about half an hour. The heart rate should increase when the baby moves in the uterus – this is a positive sign of fetal well-being.

Oxytocin challenge test. This shows how the fetal heart rate (FHR) will respond to the contractions of the uterus. A form of oxytocin – the hormone that causes the uterus to contract – is administered to the mother (she may have nipple stimulation to cause a natural release of oxytocin). When she has reached three contractions in 10 minutes, the FHR will be measured. If the FHR shows any sign of distress, the test is considered positive and, depending upon the severity of the distress, your labor may be induced or a cesarean birth may be recommended. There is a small risk that a false positive result might result in a baby being delivered prematurely.

Ultrasound scan. This test beams high-frequency soundwaves into the mother's abdomen. As the echoes bounce off different parts of the baby's body, a 'picture' of the baby in the womb is displayed on a video screen. This can be a very emotional moment. Ultrasound scans are painless and noninvasive. They can be used to:
- Check the measurements of the baby. If you are not sure about the date of your last menstrual period this is an accurate way of working out the due date of your baby.
- Confirm the number of fetuses you are carrying.
- Confirm that the pregnancy is in the uterus and not in the fallopian tubes.
- Detect physical abnormalities, especially of the fetal spine or head.
- Check the position of the placenta.
- Check that the size of the fetus is correct for the stage of development it has reached.
- Help carry out other tests and operations on the baby in the uterus.

GENETIC AND PRENATAL RISK COUNSELING

If you fall into one of the categories of people who have an increased risk of passing on a disorder, or if routine tests during pregnancy give cause for concern, your doctor may want you to undergo more extensive tests for specific problems. Prenatal risk counseling before you conceive will help you determine the risk of passing on an inherited disorder to your child, and will help you to understand the possible consequences.

If you are to undergo any of these tests during your pregnancy, it is important that you also receive detailed counseling about the particular condition and how to cope should the test be positive. Discuss your anticipated reaction with your partner before testing, as you may differ in how you feel about bringing a disabled baby into the family. Some people choose not to undergo these tests for personal reasons, and this is their right.

You should discuss your family's genetic history with your doctor before conception or during the early weeks of your pregnancy. If necessary, the doctor will refer you to a genetic counselor for specialist advice.

Those needing to seek prenatal risk counseling include:

What are genes?

A gene is a short section of a chromosome, one of the strands of DNA (deoxyribonucleic acid) found in the nucleus of virtually every cell in the body. Genes carry the coded information that directs the development and functioning of our bodies. We each inherit a combination of genes from our parents, and, except for identical twins, every person has their own, individual and entirely different combination. It is our genetic composition that determines characteristics such as hair color, build and height. Our genetic composition also determines our predisposition towards certain diseases. 'Wrong' or faulty genes inherited from parents may predispose someone to develop a particular disease such as diabetes, heart disease, cystic fibrosis or even breast cancer, as well as disorders such as Down's syndrome. Some population groups, such as Southern Mediterraneans, blacks or Asians, have a higher risk of transmitting certain specific genetic disorders such as sickle-cell anemia or thalassemia; common among Ashkenazic Jews is Tay-Sachs disease.

- couples who are blood relatives (first and second cousins)
- women over 35
- women who have been exposed to or have had a serious infection such as German measles (rubella), toxoplasmosis or chicken pox in early pregnancy
- women who have taken potentially harmful medication either long-term or early in their pregnancy
- women who have been exposed to X-rays early in the pregnancy
- women who have had a stillbirth or three or more miscarriages
- couples who have previously had a child with a birth defect such as Down's syndrome, spina bifida, mental retardation or malformed limbs
- couples with a family history of genetic disease or disorders
- women at risk of HIV infection
- couples from a group with a known genetic risk.

CHAPTER 5

PREPARING FOR CHILDBIRTH

Coping with Labor

I t is important to prepare for childbirth not only physically but also psychologically. Learning about childbirth, your options for delivery and how your body works will help to minimize any trepidation you may be experiencing. Knowledge brings with it power, confidence and courage. It is useful to attend childbirth classes as these will provide you with a chance to share your concerns and fears with your instructor and other expectant mothers. If you plan to have your baby in a maternity ward, it will help if you find out what their standard procedures are.

PRENATAL CLASSES

If you can possibly attend prenatal classes, you should, particularly if this is your first baby. They will not only prepare you for the physical and mental stresses of childbirth, but they can also familiarize you with the hospital or home procedures that you will encounter, and they will introduce you to other expectant mothers whose experiences you can share – firm friendships are often formed at prenatal classes. Most hospitals run prenatal classes, and your doctor should be able to tell you about other, private, classes that are available. Classes will help you to develop breathing and other pain-management skills, thus increasing your ability to cope with labor and delivery. They should include relaxation as well as general fitness exercises, and should teach you to recognize the onset of labor when it occurs. The course should also cover subjects such as different

Ask your partner to massage your shoulders to help you release tension.

methods of giving birth, the various forms of pain relief available, feeding your baby, and how to deal with unexpected outcomes such as prolonged labor, emergency cesarean section or even the death of a baby. Persuade your partner to accompany you – it will give him a much greater understanding of what you are going through, and will teach him how he can be useful and helpful at the birth – partners are all too often left feeling helpless and ineffective during delivery.

UNDERSTANDING THE SOURCE OF PAIN IN LABOR

Labor is a unique, very personal and very subjective experience. It is the process by which the baby, the placenta, the amniotic sac and the membranes are expelled. It involves more than just the muscular effort of the powerful uterus – it demands the strenuous participation of a woman's whole body, requiring physical stamina and emotional control.

There is no doubt that labor is painful and very hard work, but it is important to remember that the pain of labor is manageable. This pain is a necessary part of the process of vaginal birth and demands your cooperation. In order for you to help yourself manage it, you should understand the source of the pain so that you can interpret your body's signals and respond accordingly.

Contractions. Each contraction follows a wavelike pattern, starting off painlessly, increasing in intensity, peaking and then ending off painlessly. A pause or interval follows, during which time the uterus recovers and rests. Remember to relax the rest of your body when the uterus relaxes, as any extra tension may cause you unnecessary fatigue and make your labor longer and more painful.

Tension. When the muscle fibers of the uterus contract in labor there is 'tension' in the uterus. Through habit most women also tense muscles that they do not need to use in labor, such as those in the legs, pelvis, hands, feet and jaw. This actually increases the intensity of pain and may reduce your ability to breathe deeply, thus impairing your blood circulation and oxygen supply to the uterine muscles, and therefore prolonging labor. Anything that hinders the progress of labor makes it more likely that there will be a need for medical intervention or medicated forms of pain relief.

Fear-tension-pain cycle. Some women are fearful of the pain of labor. This fear may cause muscular tension, which then may increase the resistance of the cervical muscles. The contractions then become harder and longer as they try to overcome this resistance, which then increases pain, causing further fear of the contractions. Fear also causes the body to secrete adrenaline which inhibits the action of oxytocin, the hormone that initiates and maintains contractions during labor. Holding your breath is a common response to pain, which in labor will be counterproductive as it increases pain as well as diminishes both your own and your baby's oxygen supply.

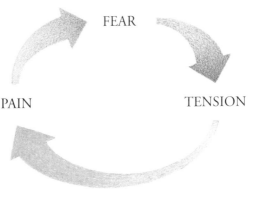

FEAR

PAIN

TENSION

LABOR-COPING SKILLS

RELAXATION SKILLS FOR LABOR

The ability to let go of tension is more important for a woman in labor than any other pain-management technique. When you first start experimenting with relaxation techniques, start in the ideal situation.

- Make sure that you will remain undisturbed while you practice, or use the time before you fall asleep at night.
- Get really comfortable.
- Lie on your side and place a pillow beneath your head and between your knees. Your body should be completely supported.

As the techniques become familiar, start practicing in less comfortable, noisier, more realistic situations – labor is not the most comfortable period, and hospitals can be very noisy. Use everyday stressful situations as a practice ground to develop your relaxation skills.

Progressive relaxation

Progressive relaxation, useful for creating better body awareness, involves lying in a comfortable position and consciously tightening one group of muscles at a time while keeping the rest of your body relaxed. The four focal points of relaxation are your face, fingers, pelvic floor and feet; with practice you will learn to constantly 'scan' your body between these points to make sure that they, as well as the muscles between them, are completely relaxed. Check your head and face, neck and shoulders, arms and hands, chest, abdomen, back, hips and buttocks, perineum, legs and knees, ankles and feet to make sure they are relaxed.

When practicing your relaxation skills *make yourself as comfortable as possible and ensure that your body is well supported with cushions.*

Progressive relaxation

To learn the technique of progressive relaxation, follow this step-by-step guide.

- Get into a comfortable position.
- Close your eyes.
- Breathe in deeply through your nose, then slowly exhale through your mouth, continuing to breathe like this throughout the practice session/contraction.
- As you inhale, imagine that the air you are inhaling is an energizing, 'life-giving' color. As you exhale, imagine that your outgoing breath is heavy and dark, carrying the tension away from your body.
- Starting at your head tighten the muscles of your face, clench your jaw, squeeze your eyes tightly shut and be aware that even your scalp feels taut.
- Hold this position for a few seconds and be aware of how you are holding your breath and of how tiring and uncomfortable this feels.
- Release this tension, and feel the difference in your muscles now. As you do this exhale and again start to breathe as described above.
- Now tighten the muscles of your neck and shoulders as you bring your shoulders up towards your ears and press the shoulder blades together at the back. Hold this position for a few seconds.
- Release the tension and exhale, and feel the difference once again.
- Tighten the muscles of the upper and lower back; at the same time press your arms in against the sides of your body. Hold for a few seconds.
- Release, and feel the difference.
- Tighten the muscles in the abdominal area, the buttocks and the pelvic floor, squeeze tightly for a few seconds and then release.
- Tense up the muscles of the legs, from the top of your thighs to the inside of the knees, your calves, ankles, and lastly your feet and toes. (Don't point your toes, but flex your feet with your toes pulled back towards your chin to prevent your calves from cramping.) Hold this tension for a few seconds and then release.
- Lastly, tense up and stiffen your whole body. Hold this position for as long as you can, and then release. (Consider how exhausted you would be if you were to tense up as much as this with every contraction!)
- Scan your body between the four focal points (face, fingers, pelvic floor and feet) to check that you are completely relaxed.

Touch relaxation

This involves your partner and requires mutual understanding and intimacy. Your partner should be able to identify where you are holding tension in your body, and touch tense areas on your body to focus your attention there. Practicing touch relaxation means that you have to work very closely with your partner, so you should both spend time doing the progressive relaxation exercise as well as touching each other in a relaxing way. As feedback is vital to the success of this method, it is important that you discuss with each other how it feels.

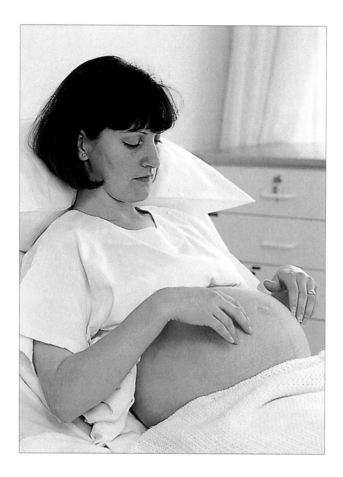

Light fingertip touching *called 'effleurage' is often very relaxing during the first stage of labor.*

Music as a relaxation tool

Music has therapeutic effects such as the reduction of anxiety, a decrease in heart rate, blood pressure and rate of respiration, as well as a decrease in the release of the stress hormones adrenaline and noradrenaline. Together these may help to speed up labor. Women who use music and/or rhythm in labor as an attention-focusing tool receive the greatest benefit as their attention is distracted from the pain. Music serves as an excellent soothing and focusing device for breathing in labor. However, beware of attempting to pace your breathing to music as this may cause an unnatural breathing pace and increase stress. Combining music and imagery is a useful way to reinforce any visualization techniques you may wish to use (see below). If you listen to the same music you used in your relaxation practice sessions, your body and mind will relax automatically whenever you hear it. Have your own cassette or CD player available during labor.

Visualization as a tool for labor

Visualization is the ability to form a very strong mental picture of an imaginary or desired state or situation. Positive visualization in labor is a powerful tool which enhances the relaxation response. It is a good idea to practice visualization together with relaxation skills throughout your pregnancy. You can imagine different things at different times during your labor.

Visualization for pain relief involves giving pain a tangible component, such as color, and then, as you exhale, imagining that you can actually see the pain leaving your body through your mouth or perhaps going out via your fingertips and toes as you become relaxed.

Use images of the cervix becoming soft and stretchy and opening around your baby's head to assist in the progress of labor. See the ring that is your cervix opening wider and wider as the contractions pull up on the uterus from the top. Help your body do the job by offering as little resistance as possible and allowing maximum relaxation. See your uterus as a pair of strong, powerful, gentle hands that are nudging and stroking your baby out of a cocoon.

To assist in your bearing-down efforts, imagine pushing against a heavy oak door with treasure behind it. You may wish to open this door on your own or use the assistance of many people to get it open. Remember that you can stop and rest as you gather strength for the next contraction or 'push on the door'. Remember, too, that it is wise to expend your energy in the right place, in other words, push where the door is most likely to open. Push in the right place – the pelvic floor – to start with, and not in your face, chest or abdomen.

Massage in labor

Touch and massage can provide pain relief and comfort. They help to reduce pain by enhancing relaxation and reducing anxiety.

Touch can be very soothing or very irritating, so establish with your partner before labor starts exactly how you like to be touched. Practice during pregnancy, when tired feet, an aching back and joints, and stiff shoulders will be relieved with a little bit of massage and tender loving care.

The way you want to be touched in labor will vary as it progresses. While you may enjoy the light, fingertip touching called 'effleurage' during the early part of labor, this will not help in the active, more challenging part. This is because light touching travels along the same nerve pathways as pain and may in fact increase your irritation and discomfort. Firmer, harder pressure or massage, as well as counterpressure, heat and cold will inhibit or modify the pain message on the way to the brain and therefore decrease the perception of pain, providing relief later in labor.

If your partner's hands become tired, ask him to use his knee to apply gentle pressure to the small of your back (left), or to roll tennis balls along your sore muscles (above).

The use of water during labor

Warm water increases relaxation and is a wonderful pain reliever during labor. Most hospitals and maternity clinics have baths and/or showers in the labor ward; a few even have large, Jacuzzi-type baths. You may still assume an upright sitting position or an all-fours position while in a bath. The gentle pummeling effect of a shower will do much to ease discomfort. The water temperature should not exceed 99–102° F (37–39° C).

Larger birthing pools may be hired if the hospital where you plan to deliver does not have one. Babies can be born into the water, but will be lifted out immediately for observation. One of the advantages of giving birth in water is that perineal tissue stretches well when wet, which may decrease the chances of an episiotomy or tearing (see pages 92–93).

ALTERED BREATHING TECHNIQUES

The breathing techniques that are taught in childbirth classes differ from our natural breathing patterns, and require a certain amount of practice before you will be familiar and comfortable with them. Because we all breathe differently, the rate, rhythm, and level of breathing will be different for each woman. It is important to take the general pattern that you are taught and to make it your own by working with it until it suits your own 'body rhythm'. If you wait until you are already in labor before trying to learn and use the breathing techniques they will be less accessible and less successful. It does not matter which breathing pattern you use, as long as it works for you. When you first begin to practice these patterns do so as often as possible and when your concentration will not be broken or disturbed.

Hyperventilation

Hyperventilation or 'panic breathing' is caused by breathing too deeply and/or too quickly. This disturbs the balance of oxygen and carbon dioxide in your blood, and you will start to feel a tingling sensation in your fingers, feet and perhaps around your lips. You will also feel light-headed and dizzy. To correct it, cup your hands around your mouth and nose or place a paper bag over your mouth and nose. Breathe in and out into your hands or the paper bag, 'rebreathing' your own air. This will increase your carbon dioxide intake, and quickly correct the imbalance.

When used with awareness, breathing becomes a natural tranquilizer, making you feel calm and relaxed. Do not expect the breathing techniques to take the pain away, however; what they will do is provide you with a focus and help to keep you relaxed, assisting your labor to progress. If the breathing is not done correctly, it may have the opposite effect. If you hold your breath or breathe too fast and unevenly (hyperventilate) during labor you will feel dizzy, tired and nervous. When you hold your breath, you diminish the supply of oxygen to the uterus and the pain of the contractions becomes more intense.

Breathing through a contraction

As a contraction starts:

◆ take a comfortable breath in and out as you acknowledge that a contraction is about to start;

◆ scan your body quickly to check that you are not holding tension anywhere. Remember to check your face, fingers, pelvic floor and feet, and all the places between these points;

◆ select a focal point and focus your attention on it;

◆ keep your tongue right behind your teeth so as to keep the saliva in the front of your mouth;

◆ start your breathing with the level you have selected, which should be the one that is working the best for you at that particular time;

◆ remember that every contraction passed means that you are one contraction closer to the end!

As the contraction ends:

◆ take a cleansing or refreshing breath, as though you are sighing and are glad that another contraction has passed;

◆ do a quick body scan and release any tension that may have built up during the last contraction;

◆ relax! Try not to anticipate the next contraction as this will only make it more difficult for you to release any tension.

Breathing for the first stage of labor

Abdominal (slow) breathing. At this level you breathe 'way down' in your abdomen. Your breathing is slow and not tiring. The idea is to breathe equal amounts of air in and out. Breathe in through your nose for a count of three, and then breathe out through your mouth for a count of three. As you breathe in be aware of your abdomen rising and imagine inflating your uterus. As you exhale, focus on your abdomen falling and imagine your uterus deflating.

Be aware of how abdominal breathing expands your abdomen, so that the uterus will have more space to expand during a contraction.

Abdominal breathing: *breathe equal amounts of air in through your nose and out through your mouth.*

Diaphragmatic (accelerated) breathing. Breathe in and out through your mouth. Your inhalation is shorter and shallower, and your exhalation is longer (breathe in for a count of two, and out for a count of four). When you exhale, imagine that you are blowing out a candle.

Diaphragmatic breathing: *breathing through your mouth, take a short breath in then a long breath out.*

Upper-chest (transition) breathing. As your labor progresses you will notice that your breathing becomes a little faster and shallower. In advanced first-stage labor you may want to start breathing very fast and find it difficult to keep your pace steady. Use this breathing pattern to maintain an even rate, to gently increase your pace and to avoid hyperventilating.

Upper-chest breathing: *take three short breaths in and out through your mouth, and then blow out hard.*

Here you should focus on the exhalation and let the inhalation occur spontaneously. Breathe out three times and then blow out hard – the 'blow' will help to prevent your pace becoming too fast. (For example, breathe: OUT-in-OUT-in-OUT-in-BLOW.)

Scrambled breathing. This breathing pattern is a variation of upper-chest breathing. It is a useful point of focus during the difficult contractions of late first-stage labor, especially if your partner calls out the variations or uses his fingers to signal what you need to do. This will distract your attention from your pain and focus your eyes and ears on your partner.

Here the pace varies between one exhalation followed by an outward 'blow' to three exhalations and then a 'blow'. (For example, breathe: OUT-in-BLOW, or OUT-in-OUT-in-OUT-in-BLOW, and so on.)

'Hu-shu' breathing. Sometimes during the late active phase of first-stage labor no breathing pattern seems to work. In this event, try the 'hu-shu' technique. The guiding principle of this pattern is 'when in doubt, blow out'. It involves a single, active expulsion of air followed by a passive or automatic inhalation (for example, breathe: HU-in-SHU-in, repeat).

Breathing for the second stage of labor

The second or expulsive stage of labor starts when the cervix is fully dilated and ends with the delivery of your baby. This is the stage of labor when you will have to bear down to push your baby out.

You will hold your breath for as long as is comfortable while you bear down, then breathe out quickly, breathe in quickly, and then bear down again. You will repeat this pattern until the contraction is over. In second-stage labor, contractions last about a minute, so you will probably bear down four to five times in a single contraction. This means that you will hold your breath and push for about six to seven seconds, four to six times for each contraction. Do not hold your breath for longer than ten seconds – you will feel the urge to take another breath about every seven seconds, and that is your body's way of telling you that it needs more oxygen. Don't worry that you won't know how long seven or ten seconds are – listen to your body signals, and ask your partner to help you. Because you do not want to lose the 'impetus' of the contraction and the ground you have covered in getting your baby through the pelvis and beyond the pelvic floor, it is important to exhale and then inhale again very quickly, taking in a small amount of air, so that you can continue to push effectively.

You may be in a semirecumbent position at this stage, with your legs drawn up towards your chest, in which case you will find it difficult to take in a large amount of air owing to the fact that your lungs are so 'crowded'. Remember that pushing your baby out is similar to having a bowel movement, and you will use similar breathing patterns and muscles: you will hold your breath, 'fix' your diaphragm, relax your pelvic floor, and push or bear down.

Remember these 'golden rules' for the second stage of labor.
◆ Only bear down with a contraction.
◆ Relax and breathe normally between contractions.

You may find it easier to remain upright during labor, with your partner's help (left). Even with a drip in place, you can assist your labor by walking around and remaining mobile (below).

- Take a cleansing or refreshing breath, and continue to use any breathing pattern you like as the contraction builds and until the pushing urge comes.
- Take a small breath in, hold it and bear down, keeping the diaphragm fixed and relaxing the pelvic floor, until you feel the need to take another breath.
- Exhale and then inhale again very quickly, fix your diaphragm, relax your pelvic floor, hold your breath and bear down.
- Do not hold your breath for too long (maximum of 10 seconds).
- Don't worry if you feel yourself slowly exhaling as you bear down.
- Don't be concerned or inhibited if you find yourself making a noise as you bear down – this is normal and may be a good coping mechanism.
- End with a cleansing or refreshing sigh!
- Relax your body between contractions, and ease out of your pushing position into a more relaxed one.

Breathing for the third stage of labor

For the delivery of the placenta your breathing returns to normal. You may be asked to give small pushes. If you are uncomfortable do not hold your breath but use the same breathing patterns you used during the first stage.

The aim during this stage is to keep you relaxed as your midwife or obstetrician checks your vagina and perineum for any tears. If you have had an episiotomy which is being repaired (see pages 92–93), lie back and breathe slowly and deeply to keep yourself relaxed. Focus on your baby and ask the midwife to help latch your baby on to your breast – this is a wonderful distraction from any 'action' at the other end of your body.

PAIN RELIEF METHODS

A small syringe is used to give a local anesthetic to numb the skin before an epidural is administered.

It is important to keep an open mind and to remain flexible about your pain relief options in labor. Labor varies greatly from one woman to another, and if it becomes long and drawn out your pain perception will change. It is important to remember that asking for pain relief is by no means a defeat. Remember that medicated forms of pain relief can be used in conjunction with other labor-coping skills.

GENERAL POINTS TO CONSIDER

- All medications will affect the baby to some extent, either directly or indirectly. This is influenced by the kind of drug used, the method of administration, the dose, and the timing of administration in relation to delivery time.
- The liver and kidneys of the newborn cannot metabolize or excrete medications at the same rate as the mother's body. This means that the effects of some medications will last longer in the baby than in the mother.

◆ Drugs will always affect your labor. Pain medication can speed up the labor process, as it promotes relaxation. However, if pain medication is given before the mother is in the active phase of first-stage labor, it may slow down labor, thereby making other forms of intervention necessary.

◆ Medications are usually given orally or intravenously by drip or injection.

◆ The majority of medications only take the edge off the pain and do not take it away altogether, so if this is the type administered to you do not expect to be entirely free of pain.

◆ Before making any decision in labor, ask your midwife or the nursing staff around you the following questions: how will this medication affect me? how will this medication affect my labor? how will this medication affect my baby? what are the alternatives? what will happen if I wait?

The handheld dial of the TENS machine makes it easy to control the amount of stimulus you receive.

TRANSCUTANEOUS ELECTRICAL NERVE STIMULATION (TENS)

This nonmedicated form of pain relief uses pulsed electrical stimulation through the skin to peripheral nerve fibers to control pain. It works by stimulating the large nerve fibers going to the brain which then block the labor pain messages from the slower, smaller nerve fibers. TENS is also thought to raise the mother's pain threshold by stimulating the release of endorphins which increases the mother's tolerance of pain and her feeling of general well-being.

The TENS unit is small and light. Four slightly sticky electrode pads are attached to the lower part of the mother's back. She controls the unit with a hand-held dial which releases an electrical impulse from these pads. This is felt as a prickly sensation on the skin. If you wish to use the TENS unit you should practice with the machine before labor.

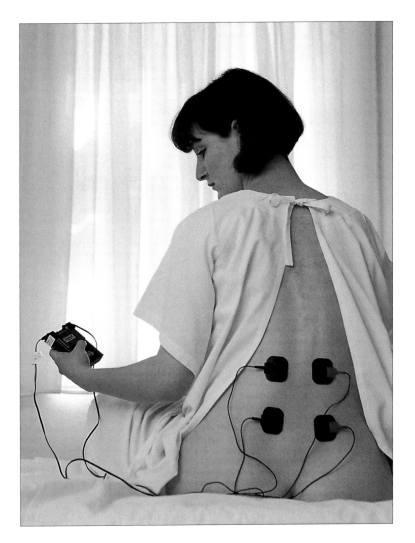

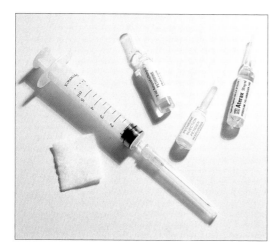

Analgesics, injected during first-stage labor, will help to reduce pain and last for about two hours.

SEDATIVES, HYPNOTICS AND TRANQUILIZERS

In early labor sedatives and hypnotics may be used to induce sleep. They have no painkilling or analgesic effect, but promote rest and relaxation. Tranquilizers may be used late in labor to reduce anxiety if the mother is very tense.

ANALGESIA

Analgesics (painkillers) reduce pain and make it more tolerable, and they aid relaxation.

Demerol or Stadol (intravenous analgesia). These drugs are commonly used in labour to promote physical and mental relaxation and to take the edge off the pain.

REGIONAL ANESTHESIA

Anesthetics eliminate pain altogether. The anesthetic is injected into a particular region of the body to block and numb the nerves supplying that region. Regional anesthetics are very popular during labor because they allow a mother to be fully conscious throughout her labor and delivery.

While your epidural is being administered your partner can support you and keep you relaxed.

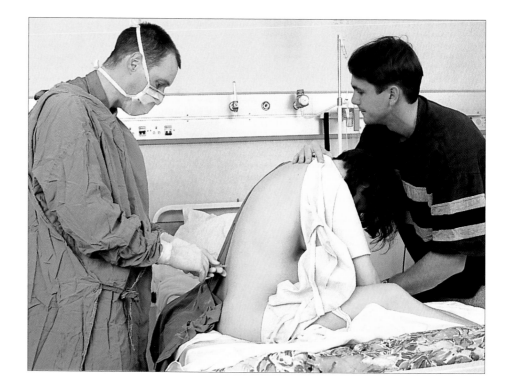

Local infiltration. This simple, highly successful technique involves an injection of a local anesthetic into the perineal tissue around the vagina during the second or third stage of labor. The injection can be given at any time, even when the baby's head is distending the perineum. It is used mainly when an episiotomy is to be performed as well as for the period after delivery when the incision or any tears are repaired.

Pudendal nerve block. The anesthetic is injected via the vagina into the pudendal nerve, close to the second stage of labor. It numbs the vagina, vulva and perineum. It takes effect quickly and lasts about one hour. It is useful for discomfort during delivery or in the case of an assisted delivery where obstetrical instruments are used.

Spinal block. This is administered late in the first stage and close to the second stage of labor. A local anesthetic is injected between the third and fourth lumbar vertebrae of the spine (see the illustration) while the mother lies on her side, and the fine needle penetrates the dura, the membrane protecting the spinal cord. The effects are felt within three to five minutes, and last for about one to one and a half hours. Sensation and power in the lower half of the body are blocked. It is often used for cesarean sections.

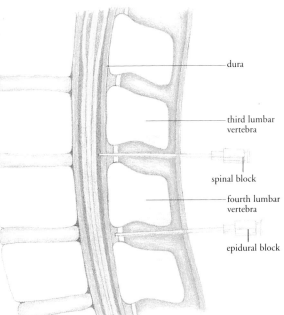

dura

third lumbar vertebra

spinal block

fourth lumbar vertebra

epidural block

In a spinal block the needle penetrates the dura, the membrane around the spinal canal, but in an epidural block it does not.

When your epidural is administered you may be asked to sit up on the side of the bed with your head bent forward (left), or you may lie on your side in a fetal position (below) – this is called a 'rainbow bend'.

Saddle block. This is a low spinal anesthetic, which is usually administered in the second stage of labor when a forceps-assisted delivery is anticipated. The procedure is the same as for a spinal block, except that the mother is required to sit upright so that the heavy anesthetic solution can gravitate downwards. It takes effect within about five minutes, and the length of time the mother sits up will determine how high up the loss of sensation is felt. The perineal muscles become relaxed and there is loss of sensation in the inner thighs and lower abdomen.

Epidural block. An epidural block is considered to be the ultimate form of anesthetic for women in labor as, unlike most other types of regional anesthesia, it can be given at any time during the first stage of labor and can extend into the second, third and fourth stage of labor. It is therefore preferred for normal labor and delivery when the effect of the anesthetic must last for three to five hours or longer. It starts to take effect within five minutes, and is totally effective within 30 minutes. It can be administered as a single-dose block in the latter stages of labor when delivery is not far off, or it can be given as a continuous infusion providing pain relief for most of the first stage of labor as well. Epidurals are best administered when labor has progressed to the active phase of the first stage and the cervix is 2–2.5 inches (5–6 cm) dilated.

GENERAL ANESTHESIA (GA)

General anesthetics are usually inhaled in gaseous form, and produce loss of consciousness. The great advantage of GA is the ease with which it is administered and its rapid effect, making it the best method in an emergency when timing is crucial. Because it renders the mother unconscious and unable to participate in her baby's birth as well as its adverse effect on the baby, this form of pain relief is rarely the first choice for normal childbirth or cesarean sections. The greatest danger of GA is the risk of the mother vomiting and breathing the contents of the stomach into the lungs, causing asphyxia. General anesthesia is administered in emergencies when the benefits outweigh the risks.

spine

vertebra

spinal block
saddle block
epidural block

nerve
pathways

Regional anesthesia may be administered to different areas of the spine. The location of the injection will determine exactly which parts of the body are anesthetized, as each site will numb different nerve pathways.

PACKING FOR THE HOSPITAL

For you
- Two front-opening nightgowns
- T-shirts and leggings (to make a change from wearing nightgowns)
- Dressing gown and slippers
- Comfortable socks (for cold feet)
- A few pairs of full, comfortable underpants or disposable panties
- Two maternity bras
- Nursing pads
- Two to three packages of maternity sanitary napkins
- Clothes to wear home afterwards
- Plastic bags in which to send home dirty laundry
- A small package of detergent

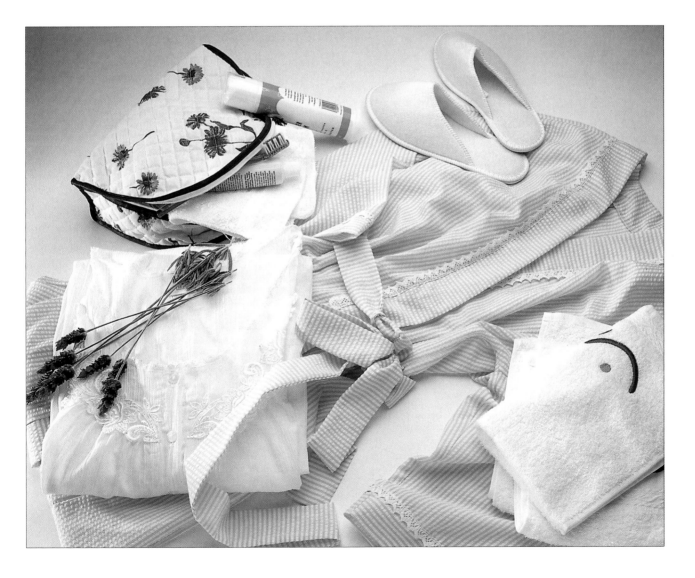

- Basic toiletries, including toothbrush, toothpaste, mouthwash, lip balm, shampoo, soap, body lotion, cotton balls, deodorant, nipple cream, etcetera
- A new face cloth
- An extra hand towel
- Tissues
- Hairbrush, clips and bands (to keep your hair out of the way)
- Hair dryer, curling iron with adapter, and so on
- Spray bottle filled with water or perfume
- Basic make-up
- Talcum powder, aromatherapy and arnica oils (for massage)
- Tennis balls (for massage of your lower back)
- Diluted natural fruit juice
- Flexible drinking straws
- A natural sponge (for sipping water)
- Hard candies
- A watch or clock with a second hand
- Paper bag (in case of hyperventilation)
- Mirror (in case you wish to see your baby's head being born)
- A small cassette or CD player (to play the music of your choice)
- Magazines or light reading material
- Camera loaded with film
- Notebook (to record your feelings and the events of your labor), writing paper and pen

Birth plan

If you have strong feelings about the way in which you wish to give birth, you may wish to draw up a birth plan. This plan needs to be communicated to your doctor or midwife and the hospital staff before labor begins. When drawing up a birth plan, do not be unrealistic in your expectations. Issues you may wish to consider include:

- routine intravenous therapy
- routine fetal heart monitoring
- eating and drinking in labor
- positioning in the first and second stages of labor
- pubic shaving
- enemas
- nonmedicated and medicated forms of pain relief
- role of and attitude to your partner
- episiotomy versus tearing
- how soon your baby can be put to your breast
- breastfeeding policies

For your baby
- Cotton balls
- Baby shampoo
- Baby soap or lotion
- Rubbing alcohol (for cleaning the umbilical cord)
- Cotton swabs (for cleaning the umbilical cord)
- Diaper rash cream
- Two packets of disposable diapers (newborn size)
- Two undershirts (newborn size)
- Two onesies (newborn size)
- Jacket (newborn size)
- Hat and booties for going home
- Blanket or shawl

CHAPTER 6

GIVING BIRTH

Labor and Delivery

Attitudes toward childbirth have changed considerably over the past 20 years, and women today tend to assume responsibility for the way in which the delivery of their baby is approached and their labor managed, instead of handing over control to their doctor or midwife. But in order to do this you must examine all the options and choose the one that best suits your needs. Remember that there is no 'right way' to have a baby, and that many factors need to be considered: some will be under your control; and others will be beyond it. Your body and your baby will together determine what happens during labor, and you will need to adopt a flexible approach. Many women desire a 'normal', uncomplicated vaginal delivery; others tell their doctor that they would prefer a high-tech cesarean delivery, and others demand a high level of pain relief. These are all valid choices – though doctors may well be unwilling to perform a cesarean delivery, for example, at your whim – provided that you know about the various options before making any decisions.

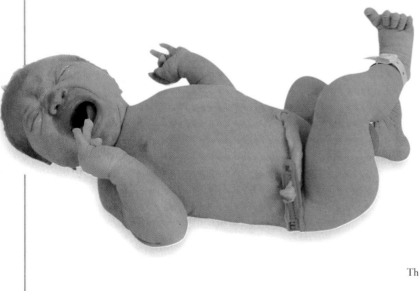

OPTIONS FOR DELIVERY

Regardless of whether you choose to have your baby in a hospital with all the advantages of modern obstetrics or to have a home birth, it is vital that you feel comfortable and safe during the delivery. Explore what options are available and think about practical issues, such as how far your home is from the hospital, what medical back-up is available in an emergency and how comfortable you and your partner feel in what may seem an unusual environment.

The loud cries of a healthy newborn baby are a welcome and positive sign.

HOME BIRTH

A home birth is often the preferred option for women who feel more relaxed and in control in a familiar environment, and with the assistance of a midwife – and of the family – it is often a sensible choice if a mother has previously had a straightforward delivery of another child and if her pregnancy has been uncomplicated. It is also possible to have a first baby at home, but the chances of complications, which may require a transfer to the hospital, are greater.

WATER BIRTH

Some women choose to give birth in water, in a bath or specially designed tub: the technique was pioneered in France by Dr. Charles Leboyer, who has given his name to the method. Immersion in water helps with relaxation, and the support that water gives makes it easier for the mother to move about and find comfortable positions; results from a large survey regarding the safety of water births are reassuring. It has been recommended that dissolved salt (2 lb 4 oz to 200 pints/1 kg per 110 litres of water) be added to the bath to minimize any remote risk of harm to the baby's lungs as a result of inhaling plain water. Often the mother only stays in the water during the first and second stage of labor: the actual delivery of the baby takes place outside the water, or – if she stays in the water – the baby's head is lifted out of the water as soon as it makes its appearance.

HOSPITAL BIRTH

The main focus of this book is on hospital births, since they are far more common than home births. But the hospital environment may be strange, unfamiliar and possibly even intimidating, so it is important that mothers familiarize themselves with standard procedures so that they can retain a sense of control and responsibility. Today, most hospitals take a flexible approach to your wishes about the control of your labor, as well as the amount of time you spend with your newborn after birth. Find out about the risks and benefits of any procedures involved in the birth process, and then decide what your needs are and how best you meet them.

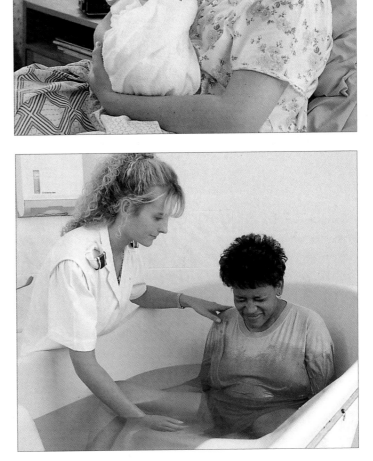

A home birth in a relaxing and familiar environment may be your first choice (top). Some women choose to go through labor in water (above); warm water increases relaxation and relieves pain.

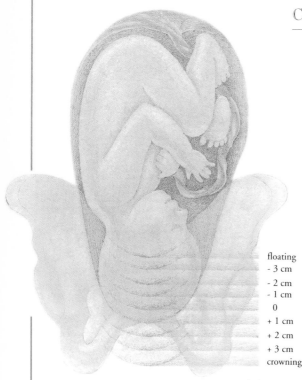

floating
- 3 cm
- 2 cm
- 1 cm
0
+ 1 cm
+ 2 cm
+ 3 cm
crowning

The station of the baby's head is determined by its exact situation in relation to the mother's pelvis. When it descends into the pelvis, the baby is said to have 'engaged'.

CHANGES LEADING UP TO LABOR

In the last weeks leading up to your expected date of delivery, you will begin to notice a few subtle changes in your body.

Lightening or engagement. This is when the head or the presenting part of the baby, which previously could be felt 'floating' above the brim of the pelvis, starts to move down into the pelvis and cannot be felt as easily as before.

Increased vaginal secretions. As your hormone levels change and your body prepares for labor, an increase in the amount of mucus secreted by the vagina is normal. As long as these secretions do not burn, itch or smell offensive they are perfectly normal.

Mucous plug or 'show'. You may have a 'show', which is the secretion of a large amount of mucus but with no other signs of labor.

Persistent backache. As your due date approaches you may find that any backache you are experiencing becomes a little worse. One woman in four experiences the pain of labour in her back so for some mothers extreme backache may be a sign that labor has started. This backache will not be eased by lying down – in fact this often makes it worse.

Braxton Hicks contractions or 'false labor'. It is normal to feel more of the 'tightening' sensations or contractions that you may have been aware of since about the 28th week of pregnancy. These are due to your uterus 'flexing its muscles' in preparation for labor. They are a prelude to first-stage labor, but at this point they merely fade away.

'Ripening' or softening of the cervix starts to occur late in pregnancy and it might thin out slightly as it becomes spongier.

SIGNS OF THE ONSET OF LABOR

It is a good idea to become familiar with some of the signs of labor so that it does not catch you by surprise. However, not every woman experiences all the signs of labor, and the start of labor does not always follow any specific pattern.

♦ A bloody 'show' (bloodstained mucus) together with contractions which may begin simultaneously or a little later.

♦ Leaking of amniotic fluid – or a gush if the membranes rupture completely. (It is vital that you go into the hospital or contact your doctor or midwife once this happens, as your labor may progress very quickly.) If the fluid or 'waters' are anything but clear, it is vital that you go to the hospital.

♦ Diarrhea accompanied by 'cramps'.

♦ A dull backache at regular intervals.

TRUE LABOR VERSUS FALSE LABOR		
Sign	**True labor**	**False labor**
Contractions	◆ May be irregular in the beginning, but will become stronger, longer and closer together (3 every 10 minutes). ◆ Walking will make them stronger. ◆ Lying down will not make them disappear. ◆ Felt in the back, radiating to the front.	◆ Irregular and short in duration. Will not increase in intensity or frequency. ◆ Walking will not make a difference. ◆ Lying down will make them go away. ◆ Usually felt in the groin area and the fundus of the uterus.
Cervix	◆ Cervix becomes soft, thins out and starts to open.	◆ Cervix may become soft, but no major changes in effacement and dilatation.
Fetus	◆ Fetus begins to move down into the pelvis.	◆ No significant change in position.

◆ Contractions which, over a number of hours, become stronger, longer and closer together.
◆ 'Period-like' pain in the lower abdomen.

As labor becomes more established, all of the above sensations will be amplified and the mother may also notice:

◆ feelings of increased pressure as the baby's head engages in the pelvis;
◆ abdominal pain that may 'pull into' the back;
◆ increased back pain and hip discomfort;
◆ pain in the groin area and the inner thighs;
◆ that her concentration is completely absorbed in dealing with the contractions and the physical signals she is experiencing.

WHEN SHOULD YOU GO TO THE HOSPITAL?

It is wonderful to stay at home in surroundings that are relaxing, comforting and familiar in the early stage of labor. When labor first starts, before your waters have broken, you may want to take a bath or a shower, walk around a little, and perhaps finish packing the last few items to take to the hospital with you (see pages 67–69).

If your labor starts in the middle of the night you may want to lie quietly and relax during the hours before you go to the hospital. This is also an excellent time to think about the skills that you have been taught (see pages 54–62) and run through them in your mind. But if you feel anxious or panicky, don't wait at home getting more and more tense: go to the hospital. It is important that you go to the hospital as soon as your waters have broken.

If you know that you are likely to have a cesarean delivery, do not eat anything and be sure to let your doctor or midwife know that you have started labor naturally. If you start labor by having a 'show', wait for some of the other signs of labor before going to the hospital (see pages 72–73).

If contractions begin, wait until they become stronger, longer and closer together, and start to time them. Time from the beginning of one contraction to the beginning of the next. In this way you know the duration of each contraction as well as the interval between them. At first, contractions are usually short, lasting from 20–30 seconds and occurring every 20–30 minutes. When they occur every five to six minutes, it is time to think about going to the hospital.

If you have had a difficult pregnancy or if you go into labor prematurely, your doctor or midwife may want you to go to the hospital immediately.

Rupture of amniotic membranes

At the end of pregnancy there is a large amount of amniotic fluid in the uterus. During the first stage of labor before the membranes rupture the waters provide a buffer between the baby and the contractions, and the amniotic fluid lying in front of the baby's head provides a cushion that protects it. Once the membranes rupture, a small amount of fluid escapes: if the membranes 'tear' high up the fluid will leak out slowly; if the membranes break low down you will feel fluid gush from the vagina. Your membranes can rupture at any stage: before labor starts, during the first stage of labor, or close to the second stage of labor. Once your waters have broken and the pressure on your cervix increases, labor usually becomes more intense. Your doctor or midwife may artificially 'break your waters' in order to speed up the progress of labor (see pages 95–96). Amniotic fluid is a light, straw color. It has a very sweet, inoffensive smell. If you notice that the fluid is greenish-brown once the waters have broken, you must advise your doctor and go to the hospital immediately. This discoloration is caused by meconium (fetal stool) which is sometimes a sign of fetal distress, and your baby's condition must be assessed immediately.

AT THE HOSPITAL

Your doctor or midwife will take a history of how your labor has progressed thus far and will then examine you to assess your progress. He or she will:

◆ take your pulse, blood pressure and temperature;
◆ palpate or feel your abdomen in order to assess the position of the baby;
◆ test a sample of your urine;
◆ listen to the baby's heart;
◆ time the duration and frequency of contractions.

He or she may also conduct a vaginal examination to assess the status of your cervix. Once your waters have broken you will have less frequent internal examinations because of the increased risk of infection.

THE STAGES OF LABOR

Although labor is one continuous process, it has four distinct stages. Each stage has its own discernable physiological characteristics.

FIRST, OR 'CERVICAL', STAGE OF LABOR

During this stage the cervix effaces (shortens and thins out) and dilates (opens up). Once the cervix has effaced, the pressure of the baby's head and the force of the uterine contractions slowly cause the cervix to dilate, until it is wide enough to allow the baby's head to pass through. Before labor the cervix

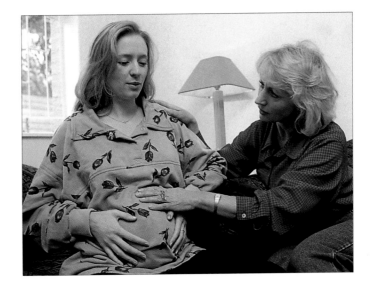

A midwife's close attention during labor will help to make you feel comfortable and confident.

A word to your labor partner

The importance of your support to the mother cannot be overemphasized. You are a vital part of the labor team and are the person most likely to see the mother through her entire labor. The more comfortable and secure you can make her feel, the more relaxed and confident she will be. Your job is to encourage, reassure and praise her, and to reinforce all the things you have learned in prenatal classes. Help her with her relaxation and breathing techniques, and suggest position changes to her. Remind her to empty her bladder as often as she can. Use any practical aids, such as tennis balls for back massage, that she has brought into the labor room with her. Try to:

- keep her relaxed;
- keep her focused;
- help her with her breathing and relaxation and coping skills;
- make suggestions rather than issuing commands or demands;
- encourage her to walk around and to keep changing her position;
- remind her to empty her bladder frequently;
- massage her;
- time her contractions; remind her that every contraction over is one closer to the end;
- hold and hug her gently;
- assist in any decision making;
- remind her to take in fluids;
- offer her a hard candy to suck, or a rinse of mouthwash if she complains of a dry mouth;
- keep her comfortable;
- tell her how excited you are to meet the baby face-to-face;
- praise her and tell her how wonderful she is!

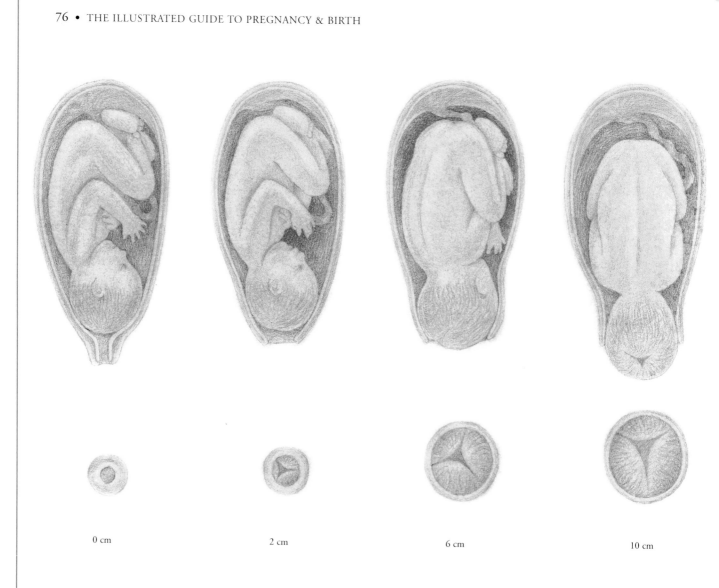

0 cm   2 cm   6 cm   10 cm

As labor progresses and the baby descends further, the cervix becomes thinner and wider until it is fully dilated.

is about 1.6 inches (4 cm) long, but after full dilatation it becomes very thin and difficult to feel. This is the longest stage and is timed from the onset of labor until the cervix is fully dilated (4 inches/10 cm). First-stage labor for a woman having her first baby usually lasts about 12 hours. For women who have previously given birth full dilatation takes about seven hours – effacement and dilatation may occur at the same time or slight dilatation may occur even before labor starts, making the progress of labor quicker.

First-stage labor is divided into two phases: the latent phase and the active phase.

Latent phase

During this early phase of labor, which usually lasts an average of seven to eight hours, your cervix dilates from 0 to 1.25 inches (0–3 cm) and contractions occur at intervals of 5–15 minutes. With each contraction the muscle fibers of the uterus pull up on the cervix, opening it wider and wider over the baby's head. The contractions become more painful as labor progresses, and you will start to use some of the skills of coping with labor that you learned in your prenatal classes.

POSITIONS FOR FIRST-STAGE LABOR

Position	Advantages	Disadvantages
◆ Walking ◆ Standing supported by partner ◆ Leaning forward against a support	◆ Gravity assists descent of baby into pelvis ◆ Encourages even pressure of head against cervix, assisting faster dilatation ◆ Increases circulation to uterus and to baby ◆ Causes stronger, more effective contractions ◆ Relieves backache	◆ May become tiring ◆ In the case of epidural anesthesia or sedation, adopting these positions is not always possible
◆ Sitting upright on a bed ◆ Semi-sitting on a bed	◆ Gravity assists descent of baby into pelvis ◆ Less tiring ◆ Less inhibiting than walking around as the bed is more private ◆ Mother is more accessible for obstetrical procedures	◆ If mother does not move around labor may be slowed down ◆ May increase backache ◆ Mother may feel like a patient instead of a participant
◆ Kneeling: on all fours on steps against bed with head in partner's lap	◆ Relieves backache ◆ Mother's back accessible for massage ◆ May assist rotation if baby is in a posterior position ◆ Reduces pressure on large blood vessels, thus increases circulation, decreases pain and blood pressure ◆ Promotes closeness with labor-support person	◆ May become uncomfortable over time ◆ May not be possible with epidural anesthesia
◆ Sitting back to front on chair with pillows	◆ Good for back labor as mother tilts forward, taking pressure off her back ◆ Relieves backache ◆ Mother's back accessible for massage ◆ Gravity assists baby's descent into pelvis	◆ Intervention is difficult

POSITIONS FOR FIRST-STAGE LABOR

Position	Advantages	Disadvantages
• Leaning forward on cushions	• Very relaxing • Relieves backache • Easy to massage mother's back	• May cause discomfort in knees over time • Difficult if anesthesia is necessary
• Squatting • Supported squatting using aids such as low stools, books or steps • Semi-sitting	• Gravity assists baby's descent • Increases diameter of pelvis, allowing baby to move down • Assists with dilatation of cervix • Relieves backache • Easy to rock or sway	• Difficult to maintain if intervention is needed • May not be possible with epidural anesthesia • May be tiring
• Knee-chest	• Used in transition to overcome pushing urge if cervix is not fully dilated • Used if cord prolapses to relieve pressure of fetal head on cord • Relieves backache • May assist baby to rotate if in a posterior position	• May not be possible with epidural anesthesia • May slow down labor • Does not enhance dilatation of cervix

Active phase

Your cervix dilates from 1.25 to 4 inches (3–10 cm) during this phase, which lasts about four to six hours in a first pregnancy. Contractions are closer together, occurring at 3–5 minute intervals, and they continue to become stronger and longer, lasting about 60 seconds, until they are almost back-to-back. You may feel the contractions in your abdomen, back and/or thighs.

Towards the end of the active phase you will go through transition. This is when your cervix is 3.25 to 4 inches (8–10 cm) dilated. The contractions now last as long as 90 seconds and are even closer together, at intervals of 1–2 minutes. You may well experience a desire to push or 'bear down' as you feel the pressure of the baby's head on the rectum. It is common to feel nauseous and shivery during transition. But although it is the most difficult part of labor to deal with, it is also very short in comparison to the rest of first-stage labor.

If your back hurts during labor it may help to sit back-to-front on a chair so that your lower back can be massaged.

SECOND, OR 'EXPULSIVE', STAGE OF LABOR

The second stage of labor starts when the cervix is fully dilated or when the baby's head becomes visible, and ends with the birth of the baby. Second-stage labor can last from 10 minutes to one hour (sometimes longer with epidural anesthesia).

The contractions of first-stage labor have dilated the cervix fully, and now the second-stage contractions, with the help of your voluntary pushing efforts, must expel the baby. Your pushing urge and the uterine expulsions are two different forces and, although they should work together, the muscles of the uterus can push the baby out on their own.

The character of the contractions changes as they now slow down in frequency to about five minutes apart. They become shorter, lasting about 60 instead of 90 seconds.

The pressure of the baby's head against the rectum and pelvic floor activates the stretch receptors in the vaginal walls and causes the involuntary pushing urge you may feel. For some women the urge to push may occur before they are fully dilated. Others do not feel any urge to bear down even though the cervix has opened fully. If this happens to you, don't worry – remember that your body is moving from one phase to another and it is quite normal for it to 'catch its breath' and slow down.

It is very helpful in second-stage labor to understand what is happening to your body and to work with the process. The baby is descending down the birth canal and is now meeting resistance from the vaginal walls. Conscious relaxation of the rectum, perineum and vagina makes this process much easier. You may find

The baby's head engages *at the beginning of first-stage labor.*

The pushing urge *is activated by the pressure of the baby's head against the rectum and pelvic floor.*

After the head *is delivered, the face will turn slowly to one side and the shoulders will line up for delivery.*

The placenta *is delivered after the baby has been born.*

yourself expending huge amounts of energy with apparently little result; however, each contraction is bringing your baby closer to you. When your contraction subsides, your baby will move back slightly and may not be easily visible, but he or she gains a little bit of ground each time.

Try to:

◆ keep as upright as possible, and use gravity to the fullest extent;

◆ open up your hips as wide as possible to facilitate the descent of your baby;

◆ remember to use your breathing techniques;

◆ push as for a bowel movement, and do not push from your face or chest;

◆ think of the words 'down' and 'open';

◆ allow your body to let go, and you will let go of your baby!

Once the baby's head has crowned you will be told to push very gently and slowly so as to ease it out. This part of the delivery is carefully controlled by the medical personnel so as to make it as easy as possible for you and your baby. The doctor or midwife will support your perineum and may apply warm, wet compresses which will help the skin to stretch to its maximum. Your doctor may perform an episiotomy at this stage (see pages 92–93). Once the head is delivered, the face slowly turns to the side it faced while still inside the uterus, and the shoulders line up to be delivered. The shoulders come out one at a time: first the top shoulder and then the bottom one. The rest of your baby's body will slip out very easily and quickly, and your newborn is delivered.

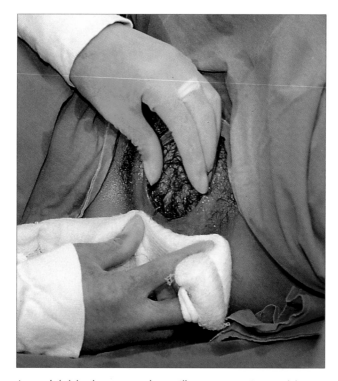

As your baby's head *crowns your doctor will support your perineum, while you push very gently and slowly.*

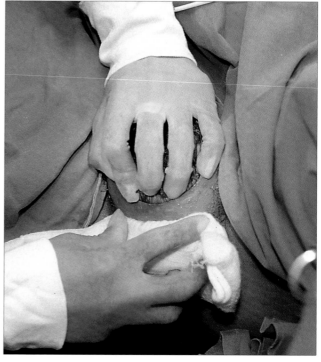

Your doctor will *help you to keep the delivery under control as the top of the baby's head slips over the perineum.*

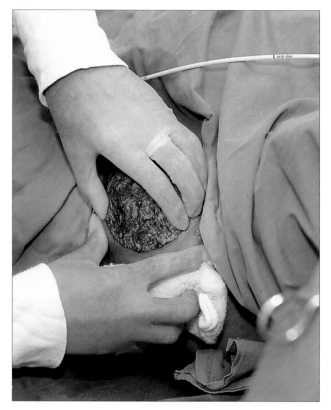

As you continue to push *the baby's brow becomes visible.*

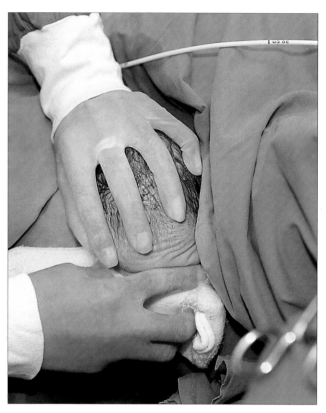

Your perineum *and the baby's head are supported.*

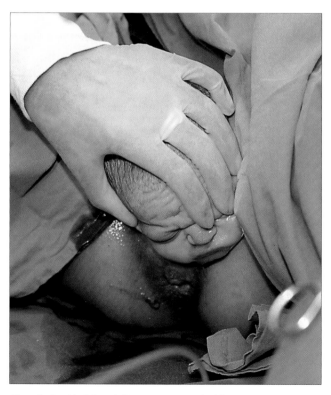

Once the head is delivered *it starts to rotate to the side.*

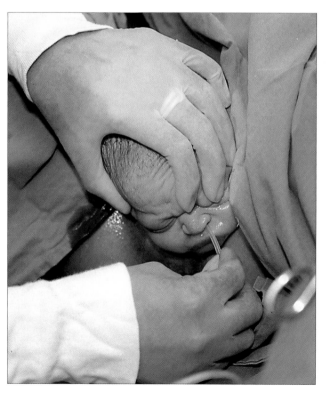

The doctor clears *the baby's airway of any mucus and meconium.*

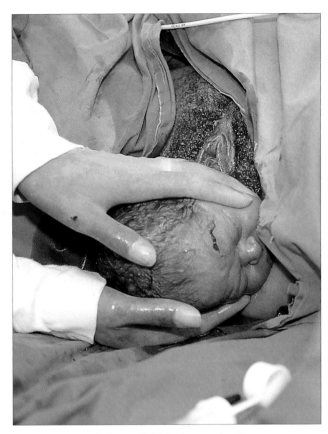

Gentle traction *is applied to your baby's head to assist the delivery.*

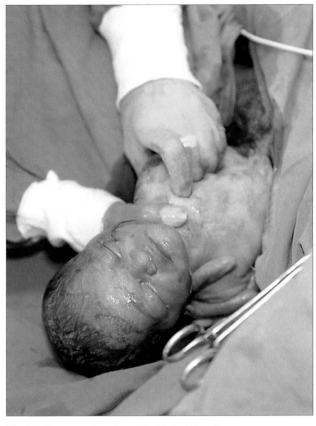

The baby is supported *as the top shoulder is delivered.*

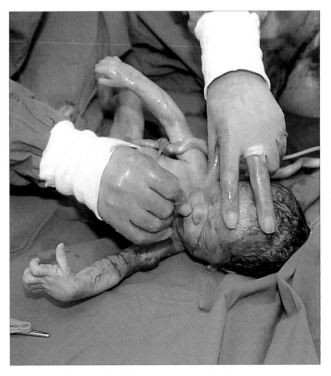

Immediately after birth *the baby's airway is again cleared.*

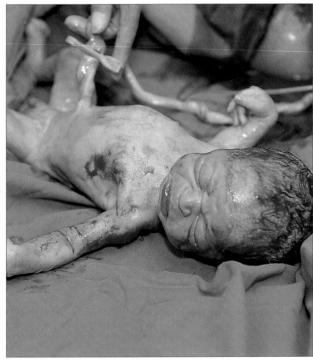

The umbilical cord *is clamped about 10 cm from the baby's abdomen.*

Cutting the cord

There are different approaches to how soon to cut the cord. Some doctors wait 3–5 minutes to allow extra oxygen to be transferred to the baby. In such cases, the baby is kept at a lower level than the uterus so that blood can flow down the cord from the placenta (very little blood flows through the cord after three minutes). Other doctors clamp and cut the cord immediately.

THE THIRD, OR 'PLACENTAL', STAGE OF LABOR

This starts once the baby is born and ends with the delivery of the placenta and membranes. It usually lasts about 15 minutes and is the shortest part of labor. As the first shoulder of the baby is delivered during

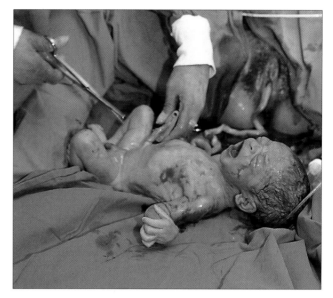

The doctor cuts the cord *between the two clamps.*

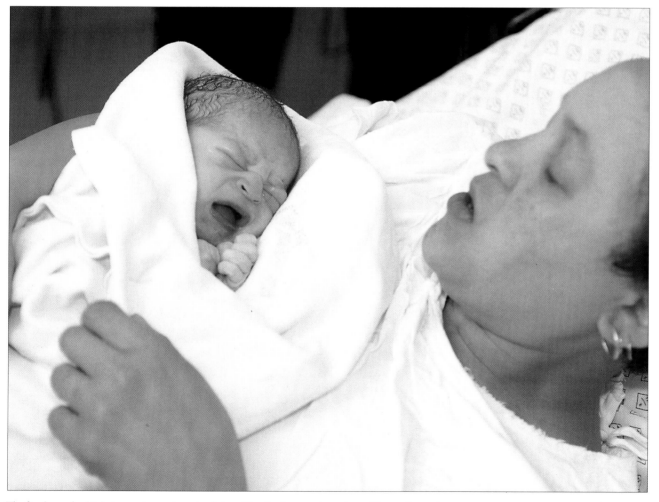

The first hour after birth *is a precious and emotional time of bonding between the mother and her newborn infant.*

second-stage labor or after the birth, the mother is usually injected with a drug such as syntocinon, which is a synthetic form of the hormone oxytocin. This causes the uterus to contract once the baby has been delivered. It is the contraction and retraction of the uterine muscle fibers that causes the placenta to detach itself from the uterus. The uterine contractions also act as 'living ligatures' by compressing the blood vessels, thereby controlling bleeding (the average amount of blood loss after third-stage labor is 4 – 9 fluid ounces/120 – 250 ml). Your doctor will gently pull the cord once the syntocinon has been administered, and at the same time press your abdomen firmly. You will feel the placenta fill the vagina, as well as a gush of blood. You will be asked to bear down once more to help expel the placenta, and once it has been delivered, the doctor will 'rub up' your abdomen to make the uterus contract even further: you may be a little sensitive, but this does not hurt.

Your doctor will then check your cervix and vagina for any tears and stitch them up immediately, and also stitch any episiotomy incisions.

THE FOURTH, OR 'RECOVERY', STAGE OF LABOR

This begins when the placenta has been delivered and includes the first hour or so after birth, when the mother's condition returns to normal and the uterus contracts. Your vital signs and vaginal discharge are monitored in case there is any hemorrhage, and you will be washed and given a clean nightgown. If you and your baby are well, it is usual to leave the new family alone for a while so that you can quietly relish your new child's arrival. Then, once your pulse, blood pressure and temperature have been recorded as normal and you have passed urine, you will be taken from the delivery room to the maternity ward to relax and feed your baby.

POSITIONS FOR LABOR AND DELIVERY

The positions you adopt during labor play a major role in your degree of comfort and the progress of labor. There are many benefits to adopting an upright position and being mobile during labor, including greater comfort, stronger, more efficient contractions, and a shorter labor. In addition, women who feel that they have participated actively in their own labor have reported a greater sense of self-confidence and control. Until you have to be on or in your bed, consider remaining upright and active. However, certain medical procedures, such as an epidural or fetal heart monitoring, will limit your ability to be mobile and upright.

WHEN YOUR DUE DATE COMES AND GOES

Your baby could be born three weeks before or two weeks after the expected date of delivery. Only 5% of babies are born on their due date: 20% are delivered before then and the majority, 75%, arrive in the ten days after their expected date of delivery. Keep your chin up and remember that you will not be pregnant forever.

POSITIONS FOR SECOND-STAGE LABOR		
Position	Advantages	Disadvantages
◆ Squatting ◆ Supported squatting	◆ Uses gravity to assist descent of baby ◆ Continuous, even pressure to dilate vagina and on perineum ◆ Encourages baby's head not to retract between contractions ◆ Increases strength of contractions ◆ Pelvic opening widens ◆ Sacrum can move back out of way ◆ No pressure on major blood vessels	◆ Tiring ◆ May feel unstable and awkward ◆ Weight of body may strain knees ◆ Difficult to change into this position from another position ◆ Doctor's view may be obscured and his or her control of birth made more difficult
◆ Lying on side	◆ No pressure on major blood vessels ◆ Comfortable, especially if baby is in posterior position ◆ Sacrum can move back out of way ◆ Relieves backache ◆ Favors rotation of baby's head	◆ Uneven pressure on pelvic floor ◆ Eliminates use of gravity ◆ Difficult for mother to see what is going on ◆ Mother may not feel she is participating enough
◆ Kneeling on all fours	◆ No pressure of baby on mother's back if baby is in posterior position ◆ Helps rotation of baby if in posterior position ◆ Easy to rock/move pelvis ◆ No pressure on sacrum ◆ Relieves backache ◆ External pressure can be applied to sacrum for pain relief	◆ Eliminates use of gravity ◆ Difficult for mother to see birth ◆ May slow delivery down
◆ Semi-recumbent	◆ Mother can see birth with aid of mirror ◆ Gravity assists in descent of baby to a degree ◆ Legs can be supported by mother, attendants or lithotomy poles ◆ Partner can see mother face to face ◆ Comfortable, widely accepted position ◆ Easy to rest between contractions ◆ Easy for mother to touch her baby	◆ Movement of sacrum is restricted by bed ◆ Uneven pressure on perineum, which may promote need for episiotomy

CESAREAN SECTION: WHY, WHEN AND WHAT?

A cesarean section is a surgical operation involving an incision through the abdominal wall and the uterus through which the baby is delivered. When the safety and well-being of the mother or the baby are at risk, a cesarean delivery is often viewed as the best alternative to a difficult vaginal delivery. Statistics show that 10–12% of all deliveries take place by cesarean, though numbers are falling. It is therefore important that all pregnant women understand why a cesarean may be performed, and what the risks and benefits are.

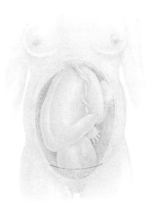

A transverse uterine incision is the most common as it is considered to be the best and safest option.

INDICATIONS FOR A CESAREAN BIRTH

Indications for cesarean birth fall into two categories: absolute, which is any condition that makes delivery via the birth canal impossible; and relative, where vaginal birth is possible but conditions are such that a cesarean section is considered to be safer for the mother and/or the baby. These indications may be caused by complications involving the mother, the baby, or the placenta.

Maternal reasons

Scar from a previous cesarean. Concern that the scarred uterus will rupture during a subsequent labor makes this the most common reason for a planned, repeat cesarean section. This is a real risk if the uterus has been cut previously in a 'classical' vertical incision. However the risk is greatly reduced with the transverse lower uterine incision that is widely used now, and selective vaginal birth is acceptably safe for both mother and baby, provided emergency facilities are available (see Vaginal Birth After Cesarean, page 91). Women who have had two or more deliveries by cesarean section are usually advised to elect for another cesarean delivery, although vaginal birth is not always out of the question. (Note: It is the direction of the uterine incision, not the skin incision, which is significant – they may differ.)

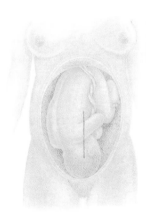

A vertical uterine incision may be made if there is a vertical scar in the uterus from a previous cesarean or if the baby must be delivered very quickly.

Dystocia (failure to progress) in labor. This is the most common reason for a first cesarean. Dystocia has many causes, among which are inefficient contractions and the inability of the cervix to dilate. If the baby's head is wider than the mother's pelvis – a condition known as cephalopelvic disproportion (CPD) – a cesarean delivery is necessary, though this is very rare. Sometimes labor may be prolonged and progress may slow down or stop completely. But slow progress does not necessarily mean dystocia: if your labor is long and drawn out you may just need to use the relaxation and positioning techniques described on pages 54, 58, 77, 78 and 85. If you try all these tactics and you still end up having a cesarean section, do not be disappointed. For many mothers a cesarean is welcome after a long, hard labor in which very little progress is being made.

Illness. Certain illnesses in late pregnancy may lead to complications for both mother and baby, making quick – sometimes even premature – delivery of the baby necessary. Such conditions include preeclampsia, diabetes, cardiac or kidney disease, herpes of the cervix and/or vulva, and chronic hypertension.

Personal preference. If a woman decides for personal reasons that she would prefer a cesarean birth, she needs to weigh up all the advantages and disadvantages of a cesarean section delivery. However, not all doctors are willing to perform a cesarean section unless there are absolute or relative indications for the procedure.

Fetal reasons

Fetal distress. This occurs when the oxygen supply to the baby through the placenta is compromised, so the heartbeat drops during or after a contraction and does not recover quickly. The degree of fetal distress is not easy to calculate, making any decision about intervention difficult. While there is a concern that modern monitoring techniques have led to doctors overdiagnosing fetal distress, the complications caused by untreated fetal distress make the problem a strong indication in favor of a cesarean section.

Fetal malposition. This is when the baby is lying in a position that is unfavorable for a vaginal birth, such as a breech presentation or a transverse or horizontal lie (see pages 97–98). While a baby in a transverse lie is always delivered by cesarean section, a breech presentation baby may be delivered vaginally. However, many obstetricians prefer to deliver a breech presentation by cesarean section as doing so is considered a safer option.

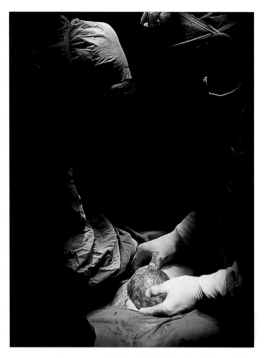

In a cesarean birth *the baby's head is delivered first.*

Placental reasons

Placenta previa (see pages 44 and 99). If the placenta mostly or fully covers the inside of the cervix, delivery by cesarean section is the only viable option. The decision is made close to the expected date of delivery: the diagnosis is made and the exact location of the placenta confirmed with an ultrasound scan (see pages 50–51).

Placenta abruptio (see pages 44 and 99). If severe, this condition means that an emergency cesarean or rapid vaginal delivery is vital, since the bleeding caused by a partially or completely separated placenta is likely to threaten the lives of both the mother and her child.

Cord prolapse (see pages 99–100). Cord prolapse also means that immediate delivery by cesarean section is vital, since the pinching of the umbilical cord between the cervix or pelvis and the baby's head or buttocks threatens the life of the baby.

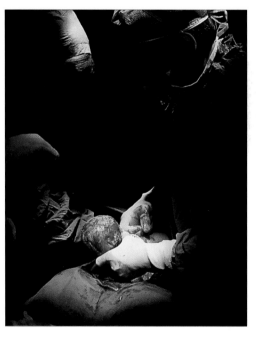

The doctor gently delivers *the shoulders of the baby.*

WHAT HAPPENS DURING A CESAREAN SECTION?
In most cases a cesarean section is performed at about 38 weeks of pregnancy, although some doctors prefer to wait for labor to start to reduce any chance of the baby being delivered too soon. Blood tests are performed to determine the maturity and well-being of the baby in order to set the date of the operation.

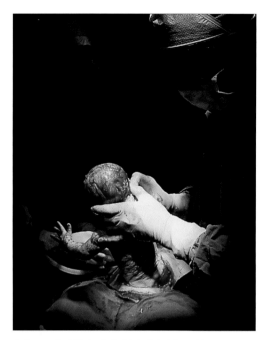

As in a vaginal birth *the baby's body is delivered last.*

You will be required to go into the hospital early on the day you are scheduled for surgery, where you will sign consent forms and provide any other information needed. You will not be allowed to eat or drink anything from about midnight until a few hours after the surgery, and you will be asked to remove all your make-up, nail polish and jewelery. Your abdomen and the top of your pubic hair will be shaved, too. In the case of an emergency cesarean, some of these procedures may be left out if there is no time for them.

In most hospitals cesarean sections are performed under regional (spinal or epidural) anesthesia, which allows you to be fully awake and alert as your baby is born (see pages 64–66). General anesthesia is usually reserved for true emergencies, when there is no time for regional anesthesia to be administered.

You will be placed on the operating table and your skin will be carefully cleaned. Sterile drapes are placed over your abdomen and only a small section of your lower abdomen will be left exposed. A vertical screen may be placed above your upper chest so that you will not be able to see the surgery: this is usually optional. Your

The newborn baby boy *gives a healthy cry as his airway is suctioned clear immediately after the birth.*

labor partner can stand at the top of the bed next to your head, if you both wish it, so that he can talk to you and keep you distracted during the initial part of the surgery. The anesthesiologist usually stays at the top of the bed and tells you what is going on and when your baby is about to be delivered.

You will feel numb from the waist downwards, and although you will not feel any pain, you will experience sensations of pulling, tugging and pressure. It is common to feel nauseous, shaky and to experience a burning sensation once the regional anesthesia has been administered and the operation has begun.

During the surgery you will be lying on your back with a wedge placed beneath one hip to 'tip' your uterus off the major blood vessels that lie behind it. This will reduce the chance that your blood pressure might become too low.

The surgeon will first cut through the skin, fat and muscle into the abdominal wall, and then through the uterus. Both incisions may be vertical or transverse, or they may differ from one another: one being vertical and the other transverse. If you have had a previous incision the surgeon usually cuts along the line of its scar. Most doctors prefer to do a 'bikini cut': this is a transverse incision just above the pubic bone (see page 86). It is not visible after the pubic hair has grown back.

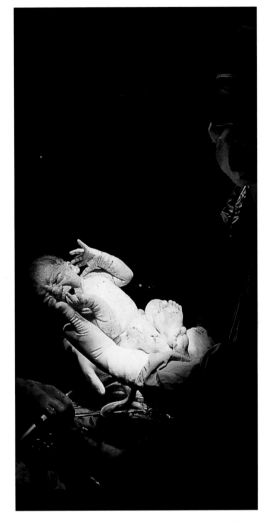

Your baby will be born about 10 minutes after the operation has started, but the entire procedure usually takes up to an hour from beginning to end. You may want the screen to be lowered at this moment so that you can see your baby being born. After the baby and placenta have been delivered the rest of the time is spent stitching up the incisions. You will usually be given syntocinon, either by drip, injection or anal suppository.

The baby's condition is assessed immediately after birth.

The pediatrician will be standing by to check the well-being of your baby and will then hand your baby to you. If the baby is taken to a special observation unit you may wish to doze off as the surgery is completed.

AFTER THE BIRTH

The father is often the first to hold the baby, and this is an emotional time for both new parents. Try to hold your baby and offer him or her a first breastfeed as soon after surgery as you can. Check on hospital policies regarding routines after surgery, and make your preferences known as soon as possible.

Once the incision has been closed you will be washed and made comfortable before being moved to the recovery area. Your vital signs, vaginal bleeding and uterus will be checked. If you have had regional anesthesia you will stay in the recovery area until sensation has returned to your legs. If you have had general anesthesia you will remain in the recovery area until you are reasonably conscious, which will take about one to two hours. Once your condition is stable you will be

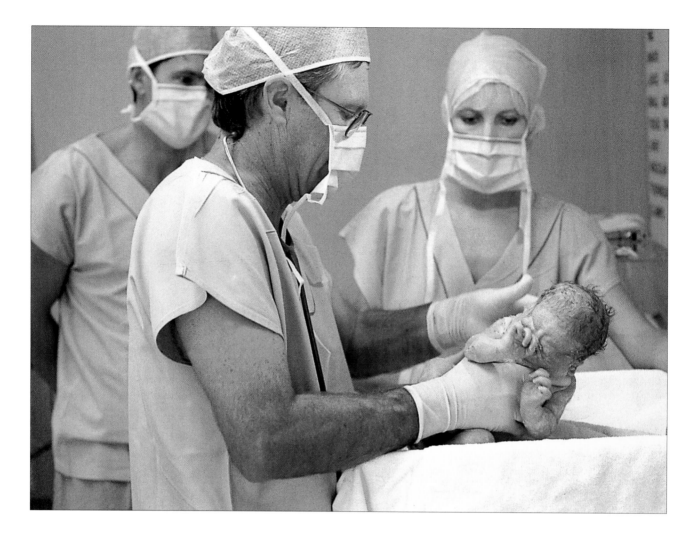

A pediatrician will examine the newborn baby in the delivery room immediately after birth.

taken to the postnatal ward where you will be made comfortable and offered painkillers. You may feel pain from your incision and from the uterine contractions caused by the syntocinon given to you after the birth. Your baby will again be closely examined by the pediatrician and then given to you.

You will be encouraged to get up and out of bed within 12 to 24 hours. Be sure to call for help the first time. Movement is the best solution to the gas and cramps that are common after abdominal surgery. Your stay in the hospital will last about four days, depending on your recovery and on your doctor's preferences. You may need some extra help at home, and it may not be advisable to undertake any demanding tasks, such as driving a car, for a few days.

If you have had an unplanned or emergency cesarean section you may have very mixed feelings about the birth of your child. You may be thrilled and excited that you and your baby are healthy and well, or you may feel cheated, angry or guilty. It is important to talk about how you are feeling in order to help yourself deal with what has happened. Try to remember that it is the health of you and your baby that is important. How you delivered your baby is not the issue: it is the years of nurturing and loving ahead of you that are the real challenge of motherhood.

VAGINAL BIRTH AFTER CESAREAN (VBAC)

Even if you have previously had a baby by cesarean section, it is still possible to attempt a vaginal birth with a subsequent pregnancy depending on the reasons for the first cesarean. A vaginal birth may be considered if:

♦ the reasons for the first cesarean, such as breech presentation or placenta previa, are not present;

♦ you have had a normal, uncomplicated pregnancy, and your labor is normal and uneventful;

♦ the previous incision in the uterus was in the transverse direction in the lower segment of the uterus (see page 86);

♦ it is a single pregnancy (not twins) and the baby is in a vertex (head down) position.

Other factors to consider when thinking about VBAC:

♦ The labor will be closely and carefully monitored.

♦ A medical team (including a pediatrician and an anesthesiologist) will be on standby for the entire labor should you require delivery by cesarean section.

♦ You will need to have intravenous therapy (see page 95) in case of possible complications.

♦ Other emergency facilities, such as access to a blood bank, must be available.

It is standard practice to allow a 'trial of labor' with a VBAC, the desired goal being a vaginal birth. You and your baby will be closely monitored and an IV drip will be inserted. In many cases an epidural will be administered. Should you or your baby show any signs of distress, your well-being will be considered above all else and the baby will be delivered by a repeat cesarean section.

Although there are many advantages to a vaginal birth over a cesarean delivery, it should be noted that a VBAC is considered to be a high-risk delivery with the main concern being that the uterus might rupture.

As the baby's father is welcomed into the operating room during a cesarean section, he is included in the birth experience and can provide support and comfort to the mother.

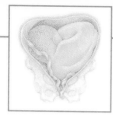

CHAPTER 7

HELP DURING LABOR

Interventions and Complications

It is perfectly possible for childbirth to be a deeply satisfying and joyful experience even if medical intervention, drugs for pain relief or a cesarean delivery become necessary. Even if you had hoped for a 'natural', uncomplicated vaginal delivery, these interventions are for the well-being of you and your baby, and if you are both healthy you should have nothing to be disturbed about. It does help, however, to understand what kind of complications may occur and what kind of obstetrical procedures and interventions may be undertaken. This will help you to make truly informed decisions and to feel that you have played an active part in the whole process. Ask the following questions before making any decision for or against intervention: How will the procedure affect my body? How will it affect my baby? How will it affect my labor? What are the alternatives? What will happen if we wait?

TYPES AND METHODS OF INTERVENTION

EPISIOTOMY

An episiotomy is a surgical incision made in the perineum (the tissue around the vagina) to enlarge the vaginal outlet when it is considered that the perineum might otherwise tear. The cut is made with scissors at the height of a contraction during second-stage labor, usually after a local anesthetic has been administered. An episiotomy is sometimes performed without anesthetic when the perineum is very thin and 'stretched out' and the nerve endings are flattened and numb.

An episiotomy may be performed:

Medical technology can help to turn even a 'difficult' delivery into a rewarding experience, with a thriving, healthy baby and mother as the end result.

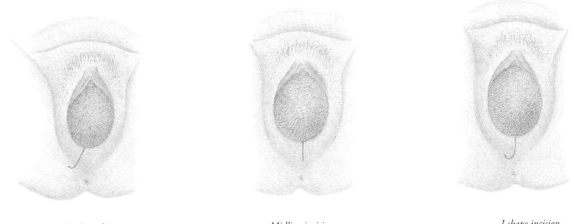

Medio-lateral incision.   *Midline incision.*   *J-shape incision.*

An episiotomy is performed at the height of a contraction in second-stage labor, when the perineum is stretched thin.

◆ because the baby's head is too large for the vaginal outlet;

◆ because the perineum has not stretched gradually or has 'thinned out' unevenly;

◆ to release the resistance supplied by the pelvic floor;

◆ if it is necessary to use forceps or vacuum (ventouse) extraction to assist the delivery;

◆ if a breech birth is being delivered vaginally.

Alternatives

◆ Adopt a position that will facilitate even pressure on the perineum, for example, a semi-upright position.

◆ Well-toned muscles stretch better than lax muscles, so keep fit generally and strengthen the pelvic floor before delivery by doing daily pelvic floor exercises (see page 36).

◆ Practice relaxing the perineum at will.

◆ Practice pushing during prenatal classes.

◆ Maintain excellent nutrition as this helps to keep the skin tissues strong.

OBSTETRIC FORCEPS

These obstetrical instruments are designed to facilitate the delivery of the baby's head at the end of second-stage labor only. They are applied when the cervix has dilated fully and the baby's head has descended into the mother's pelvis, but not far enough. Your obstetrician will determine

What about tearing?

Research does not show conclusively that episiotomy is better for the mother than tearing. On the contrary, it seems that tears do not occur as often as episiotomies are performed, and that when tears do occur they are less painful and quicker to heal than a cut. However there are instances, including forceps delivery, vaginal breech delivery and premature delivery, where episiotomy has to be performed.

It may help to minimize tearing if the mother uses appropriate, gravity-assisted positioning (see pages 77–78 and 85) and the doctor supports the perineum during second-stage labor.

Obstetric forceps assist the delivery of the baby's head. They are applied once the cervix is fully dilated.

how the baby is lying and will then insert the forceps into the vagina, one on either side of the baby's head. He or she will pull gently for about 30–40 seconds during a contraction until the baby's head is brought down to the perineum. Once the head has been delivered the forceps are taken off and the remainder of the baby's body is delivered normally.

VACUUM EXTRACTION (VENTOUSE DELIVERY)

Here a suction cap applied to the baby's scalp is used to bring down the baby's head. This cap-like device is connected to strong rubber tubing inserted into a vacuum pump, creating suction. Once the suction has been created the cap sticks to the baby's head and, with gentle pulling by the obstetrician during a contraction, together with the mother's pushing, the head is brought down.

Vacuum extraction can be used instead of forceps, especially if the baby's head is high up in the pelvis, the mother has had regional anesthesia, and an easy vaginal birth is expected.

For a ventouse delivery a suction cap is applied to the baby's scalp to pull the head down gently during a contraction.

ELECTRONIC FETAL HEART MONITOR

The fetal heart rate (FHR) is monitored frequently to assess how the baby is tolerating labor. If there is any concern about the baby's condition and the doctor or midwife feels that the baby's heart rate should be monitored continuously, you will be attached to an internal or external electronic fetal heart monitor.

The external monitor consists of two belts which are strapped across the mother's abdomen. The lower belt contains an ultrasound device to measure the FHR and the other belt, which is positioned higher up on the mother's abdomen, holds a device that measures the mother's contractions. Both devices are attached to a monitor that records the information on a graph. The electronic fetal heart monitors can be used either continuously or intermittently for 10–20 minutes every hour.

Internal fetal heart rate monitoring is done when the baby's pulse is difficult to find or if the baby moves away from the external device on the mother's abdomen. A scalp electrode is fastened to the baby's head with a small hook and connected to the monitor via thin wires.

INTRAVENOUS (IV) FLUIDS

An IV 'drip' may be necessary to:

- provide the mother with calories to keep up her energy levels if she is not allowed to eat;
- maintain adequate hydration if the mother is not allowed to have fluids by mouth;
- enable the administration of synthetic oxytocin to augment or induce labor (see below and on the following page).
- to provide a route for the immediate administration of medication in the event of an emergency, especially if the mother has an epidural anesthetic or a cesarean section.

A small plastic tube or needle is inserted into a vein in the back of the mother's hand or arm. This is connected to a bag containing the prescribed sterile fluid by a long plastic tube.

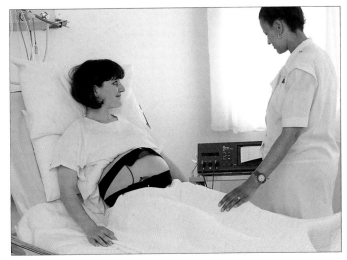

Electronic fetal heart monitoring during labor provides an early warning of fetal distress.

INDUCTION AND AUGMENTATION OF LABOR

Induction means to start labor artificially. Labor may be induced for a variety of reasons. The most common are:

- the baby is past its expected date of delivery;
- the mother has diabetes or preeclampsia;
- the membranes have ruptured but spontaneous labor has not begun;
- the baby is small for his or her gestational age and is not growing sufficiently inside the womb.

In some cases labor starts naturally but does not progress (either because the contractions are not efficient or because the membranes have ruptured without contractions starting at all), and augmentation of labor then becomes necessary. Augmentation means to 'speed up' labor.

There are a number of ways that labor can be induced or augmented:

Stripping of the membranes. Here the doctor or midwife inserts a finger between the amniotic membranes and the cervix during an internal examination. This frees the membranes from the lower part of the uterus and stimulates the release of natural prostaglandins (see below) from cells lining the uterus. It is only done if the mother's cervix is 'ripe' and ready for labor. Your doctor may prefer to try this procedure instead of AROM (see page 96), because if labor does not start the membranes are still intact and so the risk of infection and complications is reduced.

Prostaglandin. Prostaglandin is a natural hormone which softens the cervix and may trigger labor. A synthetic prostaglandin tablet or gel is inserted into the vagina

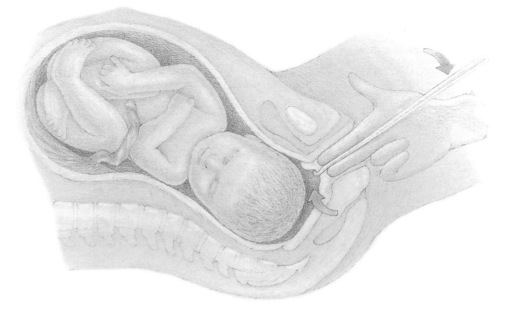

Your doctor may rupture the amniotic membranes artificially with a sterile plastic hook in order to induce or speed up labor.

near the cervix during an internal examination. The speed with which it acts depends on the state of the cervix. If the cervix is 'ripe' enough, the prostaglandin alone may be enough to start labor. It can also be used to ripen and soften the cervix in preparation for the use of syntocinon (see below).

Artificial rupture of membranes (AROM). This relatively painless procedure is done either to induce or augment labor, or in order to attach an internal fetal heart monitor if fetal distress is suspected (see pages 94–95).

A sterile plastic instrument called an amniohook is used to make a small hole in the double membranes, allowing the amniotic fluid to leak out of the vagina. The procedure is done during a vaginal examination and is more comfortable if the mother relaxes her pelvic floor. Ideally, the baby's head should have descended well into the pelvis and the cervix should be at least one inch (2 cm) dilated. The mother will be asked to bear down and the membranes will be ruptured as they 'bulge' through the cervix.

Synthetic oxytocin (syntocinon). Oxytocin is a hormone produced by your body which causes your uterus to contract during labor. Administering syntocinon has the same effect and increases the frequency and intensity of contractions if they have slowed down or stopped. It is the most common form of induction and augmentation of labor and is very successful provided that the cervix is 'ripe' and ready for labor. It can, however, make contractions more painful. Syntocinon is administered by intravenous infusion. The rate at which it is administered is controlled by an electronic infusion pump and is adjusted at 30-minute intervals.

Oxytocin is also released during sexual intercourse, so making love can be an enjoyable way of starting labor. The oxytocin released naturally during orgasm and nipple stimulation together with the prostaglandins found in semen may be enough to start labor if the cervix is 'ripe' and the uterus irritable enough. (Remember that lovemaking is not advisable once the membranes have ruptured.)

COMPLICATIONS

Complete breech.

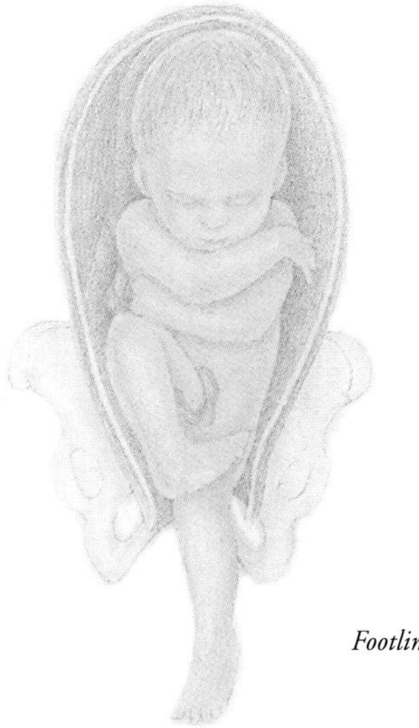

Footling breech.

Frank breech.

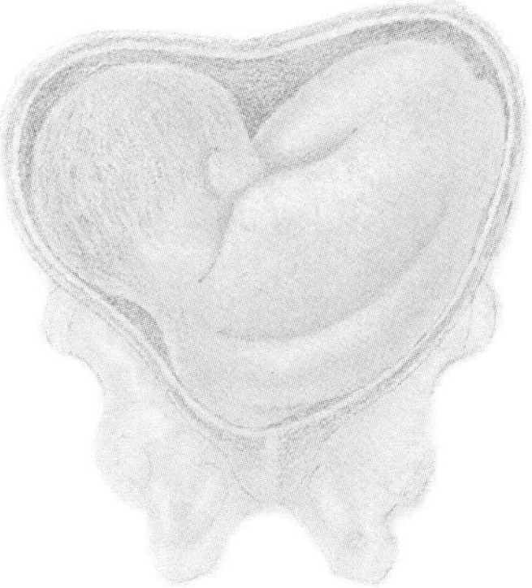

Transverse lie or shoulder presentation.

DIFFICULT PRESENTATIONS

Difficult presentations are unusual and occur in the following proportions: breech presentation, with either the buttocks, legs or feet over the cervix, occurs in 3–4% of births; face or brow presentations occur in less than 0.5% of cases; and shoulder presentation (an oblique or transverse lie) is very rare, occurring in only 0.2% of births.

Breech. Breech presentations are common in pregnancy up to 32 weeks, but most babies tend to turn automatically to a vertex presentation before their due date. The more premature the baby, the greater the likelihood of a breech birth. If your baby is still in a breech presentation after 36 weeks, your doctor may attempt to turn or rotate the baby manually to a vertex position. The baby will be monitored carefully

Difficult presentations are not common and can cause complications during labor, but a normal delivery is often possible.

as this procedure carries a risk of separation of the placenta. There is also a danger that the umbilical cord could become wrapped round the baby's neck.

Breech presentations are generally delivered vaginally, particularly if the mother has a 'roomy' pelvis and has had a previous vaginal birth; if the baby is full-term and not too large; and if the breech is a frank or complete position with the chin on the chest (the head is then said to be well flexed). However, the delivery will need careful monitoring because the head is larger than the buttocks and may need assistance as it emerges. Breech presentations increase the chance that a Caesarean section will be required.

Brow, face or shoulder. In most cases these presentations must be delivered by Caesarean section. However, a face presentation can be delivered vaginally if the chin is facing forward. The baby's face will be bruised and swollen, but as babies heal very quickly this will disappear within a few days.

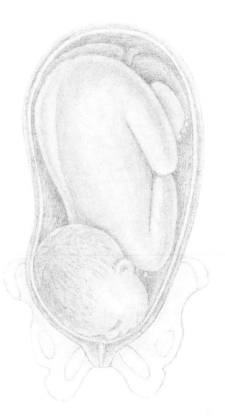

Most brow, face and shoulder *presentations are delivered by Caesarean section.*

MULTIPLE BIRTH

A multiple pregnancy and birth is more risky than a single pregnancy, and should be diagnosed long before labour and delivery. Early diagnosis has become more successful with the increased use of ultrasound. More medical assistance and intervention are needed at a multiple birth to deal with the unexpected. The tremendous growth and stretching of the uterus as well as the combined weight of the babies may cause premature labour, bringing with it the risks involved with prematurity. There is a greater likelihood of delivery by Caesarean section due to the increased risk of problems such as prematurity, prolapsed cord, early rupture of membranes, pre-eclampsia and breech or brow, face or shoulder presentation.

PLACENTAL PROBLEMS

Placenta praevia (see pages 44 and 87). If the placenta partially or fully obstructs the inside of the cervix, delivery by Caesarean section is the only viable option.

Placenta abruptio (see pages 44 and 87). If the placenta separates or peels away from the uterus the mother will bleed and the baby will be deprived of oxygen and may die. Once diagnosis of placental abruption has been made, the mother's blood volume is brought back to a stable level and delivery is done by Caesarean section, unless rapid vaginal delivery is possible.

Retained placenta. If the whole placenta or part of it is retained inside the uterus after delivery it interferes with the contractions that help to squeeze the blood vessels closed, and the placental site may haemorrhage. The doctor may be able to remove the placenta manually. This is a painful and uncomfortable procedure, after which the mother will be given an injection of syntocinon to help the uterus to contract down and stop the bleeding. If the placenta and membranes cannot be delivered manually, they are delivered surgically under general or epidural anaesthesia. Syntocinon will be administered and the mother may receive a blood transfusion if blood loss has been excessive.

Postpartum haemorrhage. Postpartum haemorrhage is excessive bleeding (one pint/500 ml or more) from the genital tract in the 24 hours following delivery, and occurs in only five percent of vaginal births. It may be due to the failure of the uterus to contract down fully with consequent bleeding from the raw placental site. Trauma to the soft tissues, for example from an episiotomy, may cause excessive bleeding too.

Postpartum haemorrhage is a potentially serious condition. To control the bleeding the uterus will be massaged to encourage it to contract, and synto-cinon will be given intravenously. If the bleeding is due to trauma to the birth canal then it will continue even after the uterus has contracted. In this case the site of bleeding will be stitched up. In severe cases, a blood transfusion will be necessary and, if the bleeding continues, a hysterectomy may have to be considered.

Prolapsed cord (see page 87) This occurs when the cord washes out with the amniotic fluid after the membranes rupture and falls below the level of the presenting part of the baby. The cord is pinched between the cervix and the baby, reducing the flow of blood and oxygen to the baby. When this

A prolapsed cord may occur if the baby is lying in a transverse position and the presenting part of the baby does not fit snugly against the cervix.

happens the cord may be visible at the vagina or can be felt on internal examination after artificial rupture of the membranes. This serious complication could cause the baby to die if delivery does not take place very quickly. In order to tip the baby away from the cervix and the cord, the mother will be placed in a knee-chest position or the foot of the bed will be raised. Pressure may also be applied to the presenting part to push it off the cord. If the cord is lying exposed outside the vagina it must be replaced gently into the vagina in order to prevent the blood vessels going into spasm. If the mother is in first-stage labor she will be delivered by cesarean; if in second-stage labor she will be delivered with the aid of forceps.

CHALLENGING LABORS

BACK LABOR

This usually occurs when the baby's back lies against the mother's back (the baby faces her abdomen). This tends to prolong labor and may distress the mother as the extreme pressure in her back causes backache. It is experienced in about one quarter of all labors and deserves special mention as this kind of labor taxes the mother to the fullest. While back labors may be tiring and the mother will require much support from her partner, she also can do a lot to help herself.

Any position that removes the weight of the baby from the mother's back will decrease her pain immediately. Movement will also help to turn the baby into a better position for birth. Kneeling on all fours will relieve backache and encourage the baby's spine to move forward, while gravity will help rotate the baby forward. While in this position the mother should sway her hips from side to side to rock her pelvis, or arch her back towards the ceiling to help lift her sacrum (lower spine) up and away from the baby's head.

Her companion at the delivery should use the heels of the hands to apply counter-pressure to the lower back to minimize backache, while fingers and thumbs can be used to apply more localized pressure. The application of ice packs alternated with heat packs or a hot cloth will also provide relief, as will a warm shower.

Epidural anesthesia will decrease the mother's distress, increase her relaxation and comfort, and allow the labor to progress a bit faster. As this will prevent her from moving around, it is important that she first tries to participate actively in her labor for as long as possible.

PRECIPITATE LABOR

A precipitate labor is one that lasts less than three hours. It is an intense, fast labor that usually occurs with very little warning. The latent phase of first-stage labor happens without the mother noticing, and the first sign that she is in labor is a long, very intense contraction as she moves into the active phase. The risk of giving birth in an inconvenient place is increased, as is the risk of injury to the mother or baby.

Should precipitate labor happen to you try to remember all the coping skills that you have learned: take deep breaths and relax. Contact your doctor or midwife and your partner or any companion as quickly as you can, and call an ambulance.

Your contractions will be very intense, and you may experience the desire to push before you are ready. Adopt the knee-chest position to help slow down the labor until you can get assistance. Lying on your side and panting to control the pushing reflexes will also help you to slow down your labor. You should inform your doctor or midwife if you have had a previous precipitate labor, as he or she may want to book you into the hospital earlier as a precaution.

PROLONGED LABOR

A prolonged labor is one that lasts longer than 24 hours. It either may be caused by a long latent phase of first-stage labor, or it may be the result of problems in the active phase of first-stage labor. Prolonged labor may tire and frustrate the mother but does not usually pose any great obstetrical problem. However, labors that slow down or even stop in the active phase of first-stage labor could lead to complications, such as maternal or fetal distress.

Delays in the latent phase of first-stage labor may be caused by the cervix not being as 'ripe' and ready for labor as the rest of the mother's body, or by regional anesthesia being administered too soon, resulting in a slowing down of labor; a posterior position of the baby (back labor) may also prolong labor. In the active phase of first-stage labor, progress may be delayed by a change in the position of the baby, by the mother's increased muscular tension and fear, by the mother lying down and ceasing to move about, by drinking alcohol, or even by a full bladder. Labor can also be prolonged if the mother's pelvis is small.

If self-help measures as well as induction or augmentation of labor have been tried but to no avail, delivery by cesarean section may be the only solution.

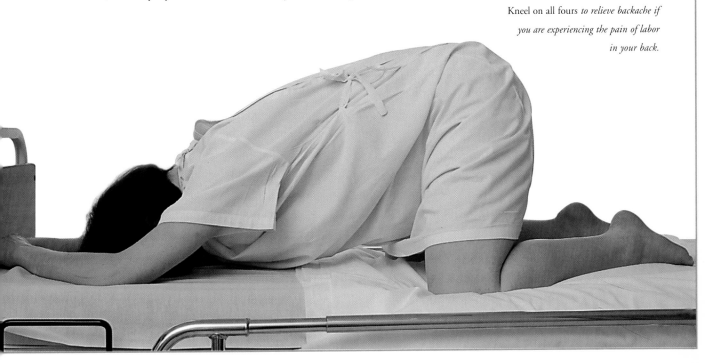

Kneel on all fours *to relieve backache if you are experiencing the pain of labor in your back.*

BABY'S FIRST WEEKS

Life After Birth

Meeting your baby face to face for the first time is a moment you will never forget. As you gaze at this tiny being you have nurtured inside your body for many months you may be surprised at the baby's appearance, and it is helpful to understand the rapid changes your newborn's body will make in the first weeks of life.

THE FIRST HOUR OF LIFE

During the first hour after birth, your child will have to make what are probably the biggest adjustments in its life.

The first few seconds in the life of the newborn are critical as the body makes the transition from being inside the uterus to being in the world outside. Within seconds of delivery the baby must breathe independently as the umbilical cord that has been the fetus's lifeline in the womb is severed. As soon as the chest is delivered and is free from the pressure of the birth canal, a vigorous baby may breathe. It is only once the newborn has taken his or her first great gasp that the skin flushes from the initial, somewhat surprising, blue-violet colour to bright red, as oxygen is carried via the lungs to the body for the first time.

As the baby settles down, the skin colour will change from lobster-scarlet to a healthy pinkish colour (depending on his genetic skin colour). The baby's cry is usually loud and fierce, and muscle tone is good.

Your baby's condition will be estimated according to the APGAR scale. This scale measures the degree of vitality of the infant, and is conducted in the first minute after birth and again at five minutes after birth. The points given for each category are added up to gain a score out of ten. While the first score may be about eight, the second score is

Your newborn baby will be born with an instinctive crawling reflex, which will disappear by the age of about three months.

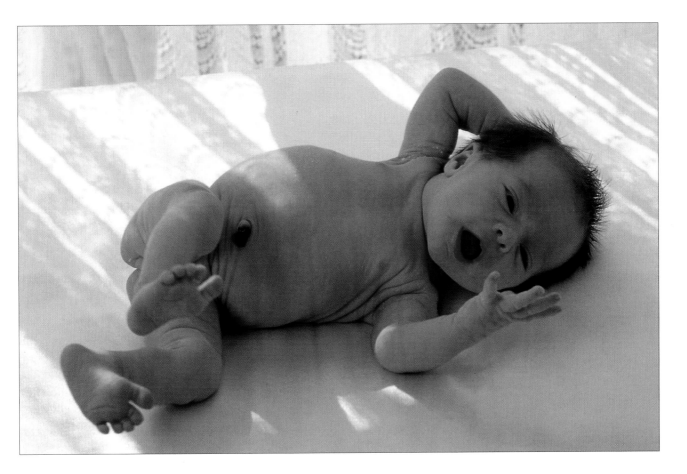

usually ten out of ten. Once the cord has been clamped and cut, the airway has been suctioned and the first APGAR test done, your newborn will be wrapped warmly and handed to you.

A newborn's temperature may be unstable at first because the baby's temperature regulation abilities are immature. Skin-to-skin contact between mother and baby will keep the baby warm, as well as providing security and contentment and laying the foundations of the all-important bond between you and your child.

Your baby's length and weight will be measured, and a routine injection of vitamin K, which is often low at birth, will be administered. Vitamin K assists blood-clotting and helps to prevent excessive neonatal bleeding. Your newborn baby will be examined by the midwife in the labour ward and at a later stage by a paediatrician. In the case of a difficult labour and delivery or Caesarean section, a paediatrician will examine the newborn immediately.

A newborn infant can only focus clearly on a face or an object at a distance of 30–45 cm.

YOUR NEWBORN BABY'S BODY

The average weight of a full-term baby is about 6–8 lbs (3–3.5 kg), and the average length is 19–22 ins (48–53 cm). The body, or just the hands and face, is covered in a white, greasy substance called vernix caseosa. This substance protects the baby's

A baby born past the due date may have dry, peeling skin because the vernix 'water-proofing' has started to dissolve before birth.

skin during pregnancy and acts as a lubricant during delivery. Vernix is gradually reabsorbed into the skin, or it can be removed during bathing of the baby.

Your baby may have a bruised, swollen face at birth, caused by the pressure of the birth canal. Most of this swelling will go away very quickly, and even marks caused by forceps will disappear by the third day.

The head of the newborn is large, being about 25% of the total body length and having a circumference of 14–15 inches (36–38 cm). In addition, it is usually elongated due to moulding (overlapping) of the unfused skull bones. Moulding is temporary and the head will look normal within a few days. As a result of pressure on the head during labor there may be some bruising and slight swelling of the scalp, but this usually disappears after two to three weeks. You will also notice the two 'soft spots' on your baby's skull, where the skull bones have not yet fused. These are the fontanelles. The anterior fontanelle on the top of the head is large and diamond-shaped and closes at about 18 months of age. The smaller, triangular-shaped posterior fontanelle is at the very back of the head and closes at about six months.

You may notice very fine, downy body hair called lanugo on the baby's back, shoulders, ears and face. It disappears within a few days. Lanugo protects the baby's skin while in the uterus.

While the eyes of dark-skinned newborns are brown, other babies are usually born with blue eyes.

The average length of a newborn baby is 19–21 inches (48–53 cm).

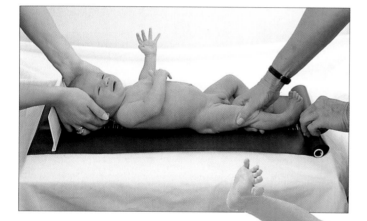

Most newborn babies weigh between 6 and 8 lbs (3–3.5 kg). About 10% of this birth weight is lost in the first few days, but they regain this weight between 10 and18 days after birth.

Your baby's head will be measured at birth to provide a reference for future growth.

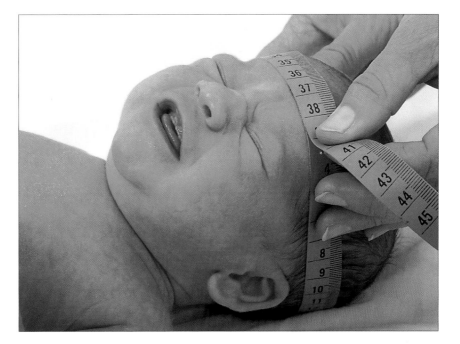

The color of the eyes may change in the first six months. Real tears will not appear when the baby cries until about three weeks of age. A cross-eyed appearance due to imprecise muscle control in the eyes is normal in the first six weeks. The baby may seem to stare in a vague, inattentive way because the eyes can only focus on close objects.

Stork bites are groups of flat, pink, dilated capillaries usually found on the nose, eyelids, forehead and in the nape of the neck. They become very noticeable when the baby cries or is tired. They usually disappear within two years.

Strawberry marks are due to blood vessels that have continued to grow. They start as a small raised red spot and gradually enlarge until they reach the size of a strawberry. They nearly always disappear by the age of five.

Port wine stains, large flat areas of red or purple skin, are permanent, however, and medical advice should be sought if they are causing concern.

Babies from black or Asian families frequently have patches of bluish skin called Mongolian spots. These look like bruises, and fade away gradually over time.

Milia, often mistaken for whiteheads, are tiny white cysts on the nose, cheeks and chin of the newborn. They are caused by blockages of the sebaceous glands, and disappear within the first few weeks of life.

It is normal for your newborn baby to have a mottled, transparent skin at first, which will improve as he or she gets older. In the first days after birth a blotchy rash appears on the body of 30–70% of all babies, usually on the back, shoulders and buttocks. It usually clears up without treatment.

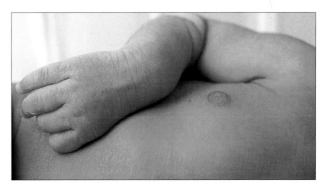

Transference of the mother's hormones during pregnancy may cause boys or girls to be born with swollen breast tissue (above) or boys to be born with a swollen scrotum (middle).

In some babies, a scaly, oily rash may develop on the scalp. This is a form of seborrheic dermatitis called cradle cap and seldom needs more than washing with a mild shampoo once a week. You should consult your doctor if it persists.

A female baby may have swollen labia from hormones passed from the mother to the baby in the uterus. Occasionally there may be a few drops of blood or a mucus

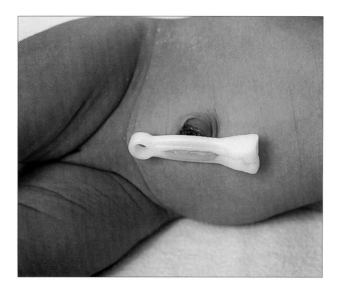

discharge. This will clear up within a few days. For the same reason, a male baby may be born with a swollen scrotum. This swelling will resolve without treatment. In some cases the testes do not descend into the scrotum until after the birth. Your health visitor will check this during a routine visit.

Male and female infants may have swollen breast tissue due to pregnancy hormones. In some cases babies may leak a little milk, commonly known as 'witches milk', from the nipples. Do not be alarmed – the condition will disappear in two or three days.

Immediately after birth the umbilical cord is bluish in colour; over the next few days it dries up, becomes darker and falls off spontaneously 7–14 days after birth.

The cord stump usually falls off 7-14 days after birth.

NEWBORN SENSES, REFLEXES AND BEHAVIOUR

Your newborn baby is a marvellous creature. Babies are not helpless, but come into this world with an amazing set of reflexes and capabilities necessary for survival. Their bodies will automatically respond to unpleasant stimuli, and rooting, sucking and swallowing are natural reflexes enabling them to eat. Reflexes will persist until voluntary control of actions is developed; in most cases this happens at around the age of three months. Your baby can see, hear, smell, taste and feel, and is especially attracted to the sights, sounds, tastes and smells of other people.

SENSES

Sight. Babies can focus clearly on a face or an object from a distance of 12–16 ins (30–45 cm), which is more

A newborn baby's grasp reflex (middle left) is so strong that the baby can cling to your finger with surprising force. When startled, newborn babies will throw out their arms and legs and stiffen their bodies (left); this is the Moro reflex.

or less the distance of your face from the baby's eyes when breastfeeding. Newborn babies love looking at faces, and will also follow a slow-moving object with their eyes. If your baby is alert and well after delivery, you will notice how he or she focuses on your face and gazes into your eyes.

Smell. Your baby has a highly developed sense of smell. Babies recognize and know the smell of their mothers, and can distinguish between the smell of their mother's milk and the milk of another mother. If you enter the room where your baby is sleeping, he or she may smell your presence and wake up, even if you are very quiet.

Taste. Babies seem to prefer sweeter foods. They respond to different tastes and will let you know their likes and dislikes in no uncertain terms. Strong flavours from food you eat will pass through to your breastmilk, which is usually sweet, and your baby will immediately notice the difference in taste.

Hearing. Babies' sense of hearing starts to develop from about 20 weeks of pregnancy, and they respond and react to sounds both inside and outside the womb. Your baby has been hearing your heartbeat and all the other sounds of your body including your voice during the pregnancy, and these familiar sounds are soothing to the newborn infant. Research has shown that a baby will suspend activity to listen to voices. A baby will react to loud, harsh noises, however, by throwing out his or her arms and crying.

Touch. Babies need to be touched in order to thrive, and your infant will enjoy being stroked, caressed and rocked about. Your baby will derive a sense of security, trust and love from being close to you, from the smell of your body and the sound of your familiar voice. Babies are programmed to respond to your touch, so touch and hold them as often as you can.

REFLEXES AND BEHAVIOUR

Rooting reflex. This reflex causes a baby to open the mouth when the cheek is stroked or touched. The baby's head will turn towards the side that is touched and search for the nipple.

Moro reflex. This demonstrates an infant's awareness of equilibrium, and can be used to assess neurological development. A sudden

The walking response lasts for one or two months before fading. If you hold your infant so that his feet are just touching the ground he will 'dance' or step for you.

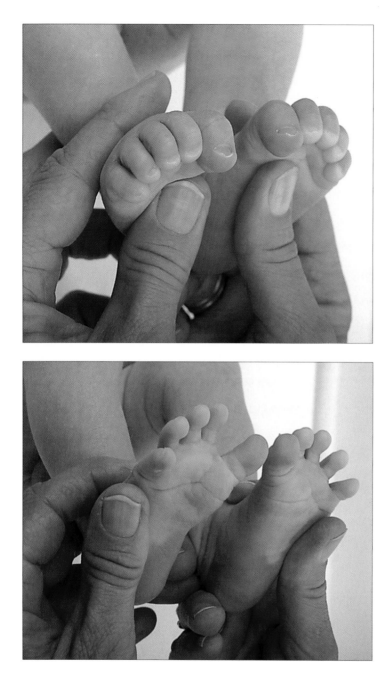

stimulus, such as a change in position or a loud noise, causes the baby to stretch out the limbs and straighten the body, then rapidly curl the limbs back towards the body, followed by crying. This reflex usually disappears after the fourth to the sixth month.

Grasp reflex. This is present at birth in both the hands and the feet of full-term infants, and causes babies to grasp any object that is placed in their hands. They will hold on briefly and then let go. This reflex disappears from the hands by the fourth month of life, and from the feet by the eighth month.

Plantar toe reflex. Your baby will curl the toes inward and downward if pressure is applied to the ball of the foot.

Babinski toe reflex. If you stroke your baby's foot from the heel up towards his toes, the toes will fan out and hyperextend. The opposite occurs when you stroke downwards.

Walking response. This is also known as the 'stepping' or 'dancing' response. If you hold the baby in an upright position with a little weight on the feet, he or she will move one foot in front of the other in a walking motion. This reflex diminishes after one to two months.

Sucking reflex. Some babies are born with a very strong sucking reflex and may have sucked their thumbs in the womb before birth. Newborn babies can grasp the nipple with their mouths and draw it in as they latch on. While all babies have the sucking reflex, suckling from the breast is a learned skill that takes time to master. This is important to remember when you first start learning to breastfeed.

The plantar toe reflex causes your baby to curl the toes in when you press the ball of the foot (top). The Babinski toe reflex makes the toes fan out when you stroke the baby's foot from the heel up (above).

Tonic neck reflex. This allows babies to rotate the head to one side when lying on their backs and to extend the arm and leg on the side they are facing into the 'fencing position'. It is a sign of gestational maturity and disappears by the fourth month of life.

Clearing airway. Your baby will make attempts to pull away a blanket placed over the face. If placed face-down on the stomach, he or she will lift the head and turn it to one side to clear the airway.

Ignore stimuli. This is the natural ability of the newborn to 'tune out' and sleep through any disturbing, repetitive noises.

JAUNDICE

Between 30% and 50% of all full-term infants, and around 80% of premature babies, develop jaundice in the second or third day after delivery; the jaundice diminishes within two weeks. Jaundice is characterized by a yellowish tinge to the skin, the whites of the eyes, the mucous membranes and the body fluids. It is caused by the inability of the baby's immature liver to deal with excess bilirubin from broken-down red blood cells, resulting in high bilirubin levels and the yellow skin color.

A visual check for jaundice can be made by pressing lightly on the infant's abdominal skin, but a blood test is the most reliable way of assessing the severity of the

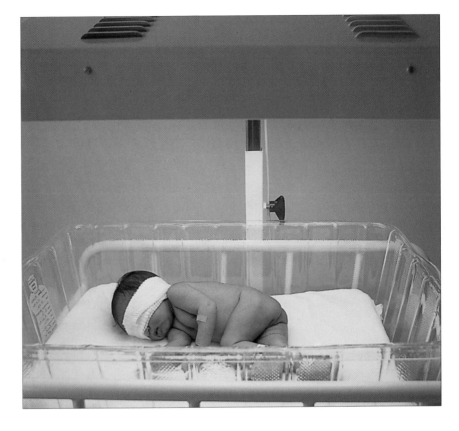

jaundice. In most cases, the jaundice is mild and clears up after about a week or ten days without treatment. However, you may be kept in the hospital for at least three or four days, until the bilirubin levels begin to fall and the baby's liver learns to cope. If, at any stage, the pediatrician feels that the bilirubin levels are too high or are still rising, your baby will be treated in the hospital with phototherapy.

Phototherapy involves placing your naked baby under bright 'bili lights' with the eyes covered. These lights help to break down the bilirubin in the skin. The baby will become very sleepy and may be difficult to wake up for a feeding, and it may be difficult to maintain the baby's interest while nursing. However, it is important to breastfeed as often as possible as this encourages the baby to have bowel movements and excrete bilirubin in this way (giving extra water is not as beneficial as a breastfeed). When it is time to feed your baby you will be allowed to take the infant out from under the lights and dress him or her. This is important for both of you, as the mother needs to have contact with her child and the infant needs the security of the mother's smell and touch.

While the sight of your baby under lights may be distressing, try not to worry, as the treatment causes no pain and will only continue until bilirubin levels have fallen to the normal range. Jaundice is usually confirmed on about the third day after delivery, when you yourself may be feeling a little sensitive and 'blue' – it is an entirely normal reaction to feel tearful at the news that your baby needs phototherapy, but remember that the baby will suffer no long-term effects and will be well enough in a few days for you both to go home.

Severely jaundiced babies are placed under bright phototherapy lights for about 48 hours to break down the excess bilirubin that gives the skin its yellowish hue. This in turn lowers the bilirubin content of the blood.

CHAPTER 9

New Motherhood

The Postpartum Weeks

The postpartum period, the first few weeks after giving birth, is an exciting, exhausting, challenging, rewarding, frustrating, tearful and happy time in your life. Do not be surprised at the range of emotions that you will go through in the early days following the birth of your child. In contrast to the slowly evolving pregnancy, your postpartum state arrives with great suddenness and, after the triumph of the birth, you may feel shell-shocked. Your feelings and emotions will range from exhaustion and confusion as you begin to appreciate the awesome nature of your new responsibilities, to excitement and joy as you start to take up the challenge of new motherhood. Once you are home make sure you eat well and drink plenty of fluid. Rest is vital in order for you to regain your strength. Do not lift heavy baths of water or over-do the housework. Try to do some simple stretching, and walk around for a little extra exercise.

As you get to know your baby over the first few days of motherhood, the bonds of love and affection between you will grow stronger.

BONDING

If you have other children *it is important to involve them in the care of their new brother or sister.*

In the first few days after the birth you and your baby will be getting to know each other. You will not have to make a conscious effort to relate to your infant – your relationship will grow through the mutual contact involved in feeding, caressing and handling. As your confidence grows, so too will the bond between you deepen.

You may feel an immediate rush of love for your child, or you may have mixed feelings as you deal with all the simultaneous changes to your body and emotions. Don't worry if you feel nothing at the time of birth. If you have had a long and hard labour, or perhaps a Caesarean, you may feel numb or disappointed for a few days.

Not everyone falls in love with their child at first sight, so do not despair. These are normal feelings and you should try not to feel guilty, but give yourself time to settle down and adjust to life after birth. The more time you spend with your baby, feeding, bathing and generally caring for the infant, the more confident you will become and the stronger your love will grow. It is also important to involve your partner in caring for the new arrival in the early days so that he too can bond with the new baby. If you have other children, try to involve them in the care of their new sibling so that they do not feel left out.

The importance of the bonds that your baby forms with you and other members of the family is hard to overstate. They provide a sense of security and stability which will make the child more adventurous and alert in the early years and can ultimately affect his or her ability to form stable relationships in adulthood. Bonding is not instinctive, however. You should interact with your baby at every opportunity – learn to interpret and respond to the baby's cries, gurgles, movements, grimaces and smiles. The baby in turn will respond to your own facial expressions, your voice and the movements you make. Playing with your baby can be a good way of interacting and strengthening and deepening the bond between you.

THE FIRST DAYS

If you are in the hospital use the first few postpartum days to learn as much as you can about caring for your baby from the nursing staff, and to rest whenever you can. You will feel tired in the first few days, so the hospital will limit your visitors to your immediate family. In most hospitals the father is allowed to visit at any time, but other visitors will have to stick to specific visiting hours. Your partner may feel neglected, so it is important to involve him in what is happening as much as possible. He too needs to cuddle and hold your baby.

Each family is different: some adjust to the arrival of a new baby with relative ease while others take longer to adapt. Preparing for change and understanding how it may affect you will help you make the necessary adjustments with a little more ease. While new mothers often say 'I can't wait to get back to normal', you need to realize that motherhood may well give you a new and different outlook on almost every aspect of life.

Physical contact is satisfying for both you and your baby and is an essential part of the bonding process.

PHYSICAL AND EMOTIONAL ADJUSTMENTS

Your body may be unrecognizable to you at first. While the effects of pregnancy on your body are gradual, the effects of giving birth are immediate. You may feel distressed at the sight of a flabby body with large breasts and stretch marks on the abdomen, but give yourself some time and care and your body may be better than it was before. You will undergo some rapid physical changes after birth.

Moving around after delivery may be sore and uncomfortable, especially if you have had a cesarean section or stitches. However, it is important to move about as often as you can as this will prevent stiffness in your muscles and will also enhance your mood as you start to feel more independent and in control.

While you are in the hospital your progress and recovery will be monitored by the nursing staff. Your doctor or midwife will visit you daily and ensure that you are feeling comfortable and confident, and will answer any questions you have.

Your blood pressure, pulse and temperature will be taken daily. Any stitches you have as well as your vaginal discharge, known as lochia, will also be checked. The amount of lochia that you pass as well as its smell and color will be observed. The height and position of the fundus (the top of the uterus) will also be measured as involution takes place. Involution is the process after birth by which the uterus returns to its normal size and place in your pelvic cavity. This takes five to six weeks. Breastfeeding speeds up involution, as every time you feed your baby the hormone oxytocin, which causes the uterus to contract, is released. When the uterus contracts it pulls down into its usual place in the pelvis. In the early days after the birth, the contractions that breastfeeding brings about can be uncomfortable, causing tension that may reduce the flow of milk.

After the birth the fundus, which will feel hard and about the size of a baseball, can be felt between the navel and pubic bone. You will be asked to rub it to encourage it to remain hard and contracted, thereby minimizing blood loss and closing off the placental site. Blood loss will be profuse (much more than in a menstrual period) in the first three to five days but will gradually reduce, stopping altogether by the fifth or sixth week when the uterus is back to normal.

It is important *to get up as soon as possible after a cesarean delivery, but avoid straining your abdomen.*

The lochia is bright red at first and gradually becomes pink and then yellowish-white or brown. It has a typical 'body' smell which is not offensive. If your lochia begins to smell offensive and your uterus starts to feel bulky and bloated, you must contact your doctor as this may be a sign of infection. You should not use tampons in the early weeks as they may cause infection. Instead, use maternity sanitary napkins, changing to ordinary sanitary napkins once your bleeding has lessened. At the end of involution the cervix will be back to its normal, prepregnancy size. Your vagina will regain its tone although the labia may appear darker and looser than before.

Your breasts will secrete colostrum (see page 123) for the first two to three days. Colostrum is the yellowish fluid that precedes breast milk. Colostrum is highly nutritious, providing a rich supply of sugar, protein, vitamins, minerals and water for the baby. It also contains antibodies from the mother, which help the baby to fend off infection and reduce the likelihood of allergies such as asthma and hay fever developing later on.

Your milk will come in between the third and fifth day after birth. Once this happens, you may find that your breasts are hard when you touch them and they may feel uncomfortable. Breastfeeding your baby as frequently as you can and without timing the feedings (flexi-feeding) will ease any 'tightness' or engorgement. Breastfeeding should not be painful and if it is, seek advice and assistance. (See pages 122–129 for further information about breastfeeding.)

If you have decided not to breastfeed, you may be given medication soon after birth to suppress lactation. You may still feel tension in the breasts and even produce a little milk. Do not express any milk from your breasts as this will only promote further milk production. Binding your breasts and using ice packs will help to reduce any discomfort that you may experience.

Enjoy the weight loss you undergo in the first couple of days. The delivery of the baby, the placenta and the amniotic fluid, as well as a large amount of water loss from your body tissues have considerably reduced your weight as well as your shape. This should be a welcome relief after the heavy and ponderous sensations of late pregnancy. You will perspire readily after birth as your body attempts to rid itself of the extra fluid accumulated during pregnancy.

Your body will undergo major hormonal changes after delivery. As the placenta is delivered estrogen and progesterone levels drop sharply, and stay low until your ovaries start to produce these hormones again. This means that you will not have a menstrual period for up to eight weeks after delivery. If you are breastfeeding you may not menstruate for several months. (You may ovulate, however, so – contrary to popular opinion – it is possible to become pregnant while you are breastfeeding). Once your periods resume they may be somewhat heavier than usual but will return to normal within a short while.

Care of stitches

If you have had a small tear or an episiotomy it is usual to feel pain and discomfort for the first few days after birth. There may even be swelling and bruising of the labia if you had an instrument-assisted delivery. You may feel as though you will never be the same again, but rest assured: your body will heal well as long as you look after it. Use these tips to ease discomfort and care for your stitches:

- Sit on the rubber 'doughnut' rings provided by the hospital to avoid putting pressure on your perineum.
- Do not sit or stand for extended periods. Lie on your side if sitting is uncomfortable.
- Warm baths will make you feel clean and refreshed. Adding a cupful of salt will help the wound to heal.
- Support your perineum with a sanitary napkin when having a bowel movement.
- Change your sanitary napkin whenever necessary.
- Keep your stitches as dry as you can.
- You may need mild analgesics and an anti-inflammatory medication to ease your pain.

If you have had any stitches you will be uncomfortably aware of your perineal area. (See the previous page for further information about caring for your stitches.) Sitting and moving around may be uncomfortable, and the very thought of passing a bowel motion terrifying. Hemorrhoids (see page 41) are common after delivery and can be extremely uncomfortable, but they will disappear after a few days. A warm bath, into which you have mixed a cupful of salt, will also increase your comfort, especially if you have passed a stool. Most stitches dissolve on their own, but some doctors use suturing material that must be removed after five days.

It is important to avoid constipation. Eat high-fiber foods and fresh fruits and vegetables from day one to encourage normal bowel movements. You may be given a 'cocktail' on the third day to encourage your bowels to work without causing diarrhea. Drink plenty of water instead of tea and coffee. Respond to your bowel signals as soon as you can. Do not strain on the toilet, and support your perineum with a clean sanitary napkin if this makes you feel more comfortable. Make sure you continue to do the pelvic floor muscle exercises described on page 36.

BRINGING YOUR BABY BACK HOME

Once you get back home, try to get some extra help for the first few weeks. It is essential to find time for rest and relaxation. If possible, have your partner take some time off work so that he can be at home with you. Accept help from family and friends. Ask close friends to help you with shopping and cooking. Your most important task now is to care for yourself and your baby: having a tidy, showcase home and supper on the table on time is not high on your list of priorities at the moment.

One of the major adjustments you will have to make is to get used to the disruption of your sleep. Newborn babies sleep a lot but only for short periods at a time. They wake up every two to three hours for a feeding, and breastfed babies will wake up more frequently than formula-fed babies. Ongoing sleep disturbance will wear you down, making you irritable, cross and short-tempered. To help yourself cope, sleep when your baby does and don't feel that you have to keep going back to household chores. You have a natural 'interrupt' mechanism that will wake you if your baby cries. Many new parents find it easier to have the baby in bed with them at night. This also provides them with an opportunity to spend time cuddling their new baby. Don't worry about falling asleep while breastfeeding: you won't smother the baby in your sleep (but don't sleep with your baby if you have drunk too much).

Limit your visitors in your first days home: although they mean well they will tire and exhaust you. Take your phone off the hook and tape a 'Do Not Disturb!' note to the front door when you want to take a nap or feed your baby undisturbed. In addition, let someone you trust look after your baby from time to time – this short break from your parenting duties can be a wonderful boost.

Make sure that you continue to eat a well-balanced diet which includes plenty of fresh fruits and vegetables. If you are breastfeeding ensure that you drink plenty of fluids.

Lack of good, restful sleep coupled with hormonal changes and recuperation from the stress of birth may make you feel tearful and depressed from time to time. These 'baby blues' are normal and are part of adapting to your new role. True post-natal depression, however, is more serious (see page 118) and should not be ignored.

MAKING LOVE AFTER HAVING A BABY

There are no rules as to when a couple will be able to resume their sex life. This is a very personal issue that needs to be approached with sensitivity and understanding. Some couples will resume sexual intercourse very soon after birth, especially if the mother has had no stitches or abdominal surgery. Other couples take longer. Lack of sleep, a sore perineum, a demanding baby or just general fatigue as the mother recovers from birth do not do much to enhance the libido. It used to be suggested that a couple wait until the six-week check-up before resuming intercourse. However, some couples need and want to make love before this time is up. If you have healed well and there is no vaginal discharge, you may be ready to start. Be very slow and gentle at first and do not be concerned if there are no 'fireworks'. Tension and slight discomfort may interfere with your full enjoyment of intercourse. If you are breastfeeding you may be surprised to find that you will leak milk from your breasts when you experience orgasm and release the hormone oxytocin – this is perfectly normal. It is important to use an external form of lubrication (such as K-Y Jelly or aqueous cream) in the beginning, as the hormonal changes you are undergoing make vaginal dryness normal. Even though you may be breastfeeding and may not have had a period, it is possible to become pregnant. Discuss contraception with your doctor right after the birth and do not wait until your six-week check-up. If you have any other concerns or fears about intercourse be sure to mention these as well. If you have not yet decided on a long-term contraceptive method, use condoms until you have done so.

POSTNATAL DEPRESSION

Most women accept the fact that the postpartum period has the potential to cause 'madness and sadness'. Some women experience this briefly and very lightly, while others suffer months of misery and pain. Women with a history of depressive episodes or emotional difficulties are at a higher risk of developing postnatal depression. There appears to be a combination of factors that may lead to maternal depression. These include hormonal changes, the emotional and physical stress of birth, the stress of caring for a newborn baby, and sleep disturbances.

Nutrition

Make sure that you continue to eat a well-balanced diet and drink plenty of water (see pages 26–29). Do not skip meals or eat foods that are high in fat and sugars. Any weight reduction should be monitored, and dieting is not recommended at this time, especially if you are breastfeeding. Remember to take things slowly and do not try to do too much too soon. Do not forget that your health and that of your family come first.

Decide on a method of contraception before resuming intercourse. Even if your periods have not returned, it is still possible to get pregnant during the weeks after birth.

Postnatal depression falls into four categories:

Maternal or baby blues. Baby blues are characterized by crying, anxiety over the baby, confusion, irritability and fatigue. They occur on about day three, and are very common. As many as 80% of new mothers experience some form of emotional upset shortly after the birth. The 'baby blues' usually last no more than a few days, and sometimes only a few hours. Although there are no clear statistics, it is thought that the father may also suffer from a form of postnatal depression as the realization of his new responsibilities causes an emotional reaction.

Depression. About 10% of women develop a more severe form of depressive illness than 'baby blues', beginning a week or more after the birth. This involves a pattern of depression that becomes evident in the form of prevailing despondency, tearfulness, feelings of inadequacy and an inability to cope, fears about the health of the baby, increased irritability and undue fatigue. Appetite disturbance and a decrease in sexual interest are also common. If unrecognized and left untreated, this form of depression may progress to severe depression.

Severe depression. This occurs at more or less the same rate and takes the same form as severe depression in the rest of the population. The symptoms include feelings of permeating sadness, guilt, pessimism, anxiety, agitation, as well as loss of libido, sleep disturbances, weight disturbances, self-neglect and an inability to concentrate. The development of any severe emotional disorder within a year of giving birth is still considered to be related to the birth.

Postnatal or puerperal psychosis. This is rare, and requires extensive emotional and practical support from family, friends and health professionals. Symptoms are similar to those of severe depression, but may be more marked. The mother may become increasingly withdrawn, appear confused, and experience hallucinations and delusions. It is vital that she and her family seek help, which will involve medication and counseling. She may need to spend some time in the hospital.

Coping with depression

First and foremost, understanding and emotional support for the mother from friends and family are necessary. She cannot 'snap out of it' or 'pull herself together'! By giving birth to a baby she has undergone a considerable amount of physical stress that sometimes may cause a biochemical imbalance in her body. It is important that any mother affected by depression feels free to share her emotions and state of mind, and is not made to feel that, because she is finding the job of mothering hard to deal with at times, she is 'weak' or inadequate.

As a new mother it is important to talk about and express your fears and concerns. It is helpful to retain some perspective of the situation and this is best done by sharing your feelings with others. If the problem becomes more serious or complicated and the help and support of friends and family is not enough, then seek the help of a professional such as a psychologist, psychiatrist, midwife, social worker or doctor. If the problem is severe then treatment in the form of medication as well as professional counseling may be necessary. Remember that depression is an illness and needs to be dealt with as such.

GETTING BACK INTO SHAPE

In order to regain your strength and vitality it is important to start doing a little body-conditioning exercise, although do not overdo it or skimp on any of the rest and relaxation you will be needing.

A brisk walk with your baby in a stroller or carriage will get you out and about and will help to banish any frustration or fatigue. Doing a few simple exercises in the hospital and at home will help you regain your strength and leave you better able to cope, emotionally and physically, with the demands of motherhood. You can carry on doing the exercises you learned in the prenatal period (see pages 32–36).

Neck exercises will help alleviate the tightness and tension you feel as a result of breastfeeding, carrying the baby and general fatigue. Basic leg stretches and leg sliding will help tone and strengthen the leg muscles. Start doing pelvic floor exercises (see page 36) as soon as possible after the birth, even if you find them difficult. Hold the squeeze for two to three seconds at first, gradually work up to a count of five, and repeat in sets of three or four squeezes throughout the day. The pelvic tilt (see page 33) is another useful exercise to tone and strengthen the abdominal muscles and relieve backache. It is important to do exercises to strengthen your abdominal muscles, but do not forget to check for separation (see page 32). An easy abdominal exercise, which can be done while you are lying on your back, or while you are standing or sitting, involves squeezing the abdominal muscles and holding for ten seconds – this is equivalent to one sit-up: keep your hands on your tummy so that you feel the muscles tightening and exhale as you contract. Start with five contractions a day and gradually progress to ten.

The following exercises are new ones, and will do much to increase your vitality and strengthen your abdominal muscles, your lower back and your hip flexors.

You may want to start going to postnatal exercise classes three to six weeks after the birth of your baby. The advantages of these classes are that, besides being taught by qualified instructors who are experts at getting you going again, you will be able to take your baby with you and meet other mothers. In this way you can share your experiences and offer support to one another.

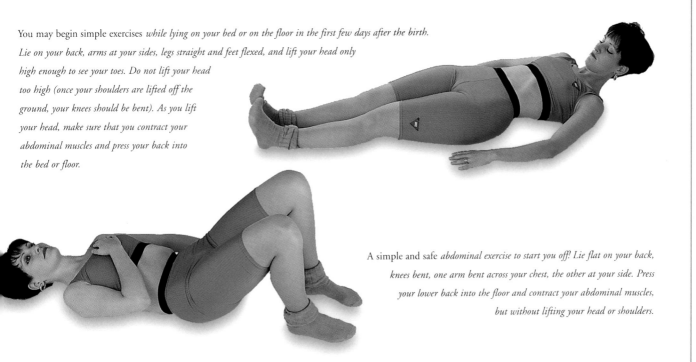

You may begin simple exercises *while lying on your bed or on the floor in the first few days after the birth. Lie on your back, arms at your sides, legs straight and feet flexed, and lift your head only high enough to see your toes. Do not lift your head too high (once your shoulders are lifted off the ground, your knees should be bent). As you lift your head, make sure that you contract your abdominal muscles and press your back into the bed or floor.*

A simple and safe *abdominal exercise to start you off! Lie flat on your back, knees bent, one arm bent across your chest, the other at your side. Press your lower back into the floor and contract your abdominal muscles, but without lifting your head or shoulders.*

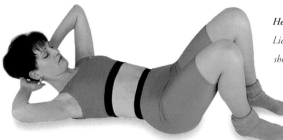

Head and shoulder curl-up 1

Lie on your back with your knees bent at 90º and shoulder-width apart. Lift your head and shoulders just off the ground, exhaling as you do so. Pause as you look between your knees, and then lower your head slowly, inhaling on the way down. Relax and then repeat five to ten times twice a day. If you are tempted to push your head up with your hands, rest them over your ears.

Head and shoulder curl-up 2

This is an exercise for when you are feeling stronger. Do this in the same way as the previous exercise, but lift higher off the ground so that you can feel your stomach muscles working. Start with three repetitions twice a day and progress to ten. Be careful not to pull your head up with your hands as this may hurt your neck.

Sitback

This exercise should only be done when you can do the head and shoulder curl-up exercise above with 10 repetitions and no feeling of strain on the muscles. A wedge and a broomstick will give you extra support. As shown below left, sit on the floor with bent knees, with the stick held underneath your knees and the wedge, if using, behind you. Lean back slowly, curling your torso forward slightly as you squeeze the abdominals (below right), and exhaling as you do so. Lean back only as far as you can without losing control or until you feel the wedge against your back, pause, and then straighten up, at the same time inhaling. Do not forget to breathe out as you contract your abdominals and breathe in as you release them.

Diagonal curl-up

This will trim up your waist by strengthening your diagonal abdominal muscles. Lie in the same position as for the curl-up exercises, but place your right hand at the side of your head and your left arm at your side. Place your left ankle across your right knee. Now bring the elbow of the supporting right arm across your body towards the left knee. As you lift your head, press your back well into the floor and tuck your chin in. Pause for a count of three and lower slowly, inhaling as you do so. Repeat five to ten times on each side. Repeat on both sides twice a day.

This exercise stretches and lengthens *the shortened muscles in the lower and upper back and alleviates any tension and tightness in these areas. Sit on the edge of a chair with your feet hip-width apart and flat on the ground. Bend slowly forwards, dropping your arms between your legs, until your head is lower than your hips, breathing out as you go down. Hold for five seconds and then reverse the movement, uncurling the spine from the hips gradually up to the head, breathing in as you rise.*

Including your baby *in your exercise routine is fun for both of you: he or she has your attention and feels involved in what you are doing and, at the same time, you are not distracted or worried that he may be fretting. Simple exercises such as the head and shoulder curl-up are ideally suited to doing with your child.*

CHAPTER 10

PRACTICAL PARENTING

Hints and Tips for the Early Days

Try to relax and enjoy these early days as your baby's personality unfolds before you. Initially, caring for this new addition to the family will absorb you physically, mentally and emotionally, as the baby is completely dependent upon you. You may experience a few minor upsets and problems in these early days, but reading and asking questions will help you to recognize and prepare for them. Before you know it your infant will be smiling and gurgling at you, and trying to let you know how important you are to him or her.

FEEDING YOUR BABY

One of the first decisions facing you as a new mother is how you are going to feed your child. It is best to make this decision before the birth, so that if you plan to breastfeed you can take advantage of those precious moments after birth to put your baby to your breast. Many women are determined to breastfeed; other women, for personal or medical reasons, decide to formula-feed their babies by bottle. Before making up your mind you should inform yourself fully of the advantages and disadvantages of the different options.

It is important to burp your baby properly after each feeding. Hold the baby against your shoulder with one hand and support the child's bottom with the other. Firmly but gently rub or pat the baby's back in an upward direction.

GUIDE TO BREASTFEEDING

Advantages for your baby

Breastfeeding has distinct health advantages for your baby as colostrum (the concentrated milk produced in the first few days after birth) and breast milk both contain antibodies to protect your baby from viral, gastrointestinal and respiratory infections. Breast milk is the perfect food as it is easily digestible and has all the nutrients a baby needs. Recent discoveries show that there are certain amino acids and fats in breast milk that contribute to the optimal development of the brain, 65% of which occurs in the first year. Breastfed babies have a reduced chance of developing allergies, obesity or heart disease as adults. Breast milk has the unique ability to change composition during a feeding and as your baby gets older: milk needed by and produced for a premature infant will be different to that for a full-term baby, and changes again to meet the nutritional requirements of an older baby.

Advantages for the mother

There are several advantages of breastfeeding for the mother, including rapid involution of the uterus after birth (see page 114) and faster weight loss of the reserves that were 'stocked' during pregnancy. Breastfeeding is practical, convenient, and, unlike bottle-feeding, does not require extensive preparation and sterilization. Breast milk is free and, provided your baby has frequent access to the breast, it will never run out. Breastfeeding at night is quicker and easier than bottle-feedings; this means that the baby can be fed before he or she has time to become fully awake, and will go back to sleep more easily. In addition, breastfed babies' stools and vomit smell less offensive.

The composition of breast milk

In the early days after birth your baby will get three different types of breast milk during a single breastfeeding.

Colostrum. Colostrum is secreted during the first two to five days after birth. It is very concentrated, containing water, sugar, protein, vitamins and minerals in just the right proportions to take care of your baby's nutritional needs, and it is rich in valuable antibodies. The nutritional value of 5 ml of colostrum is equal to 30 ml of mature breast milk. During the next three weeks the milk produced changes and is known as transitional milk. Mature milk appears after about 30 days.

NUTRIENTS/100 ML BREAST MILK VERSUS NUTRIENTS/100 ML MODIFIED COW'S MILK NEWBORN FORMULA		
Nutrient	Breast milk	Newborn formula
Protein	1.2 g	3.3 g
Carbohydrate (lactose)	7.0 g	4.8 g
Fat	3.8 g	3.7 g
Sodium	15 mg	58 mg
Potassium	55 mg	138 mg
Calcium	33 mg	125 mg
Phosphorus	15 mg	96 mg
Magnesium	4 mg	12 mg

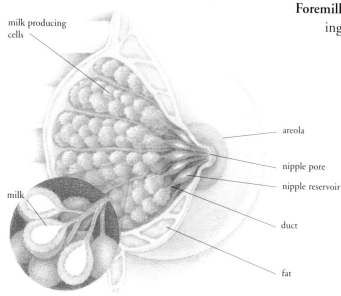

milk producing
cells

areola

nipple pore

nipple reservoir

milk

duct

fat

Cross-section of a lactating breast.

Foremilk. This – the first milk to come through during a feeding – satisfies your baby's thirst. It consists mostly of water, protein and water-soluble vitamins, and is low in fat and carbohydrates. This milk gathers in the reservoirs behind the nipple between feedings.

Hindmilk. The richer hindmilk is released towards the end of the feeding with the assistance of the mother's let-down reflex which works continuously throughout the entire feeding (see below). This milk is made up of fats and carbohydrates and satisfies your baby's hunger. If the feeding ends too soon your baby will be denied the hindmilk and, even though her thirst will be quenched, she will still be hungry.

How breastfeeding works

Your baby, correctly latched on, suckles on the breast. This causes a nerve impulse to travel to the brain with the message to produce milk. The brain responds by secreting the hormone prolactin, which stimulates milk production in the breast. Suckling also stimulates the production of the hormone oxytocin, which causes the milk-producing cells in your breasts to drain their milk into the reservoirs in the nipple area. This let-down reflex causes milk to flow into the baby's mouth when he or she suckles. If the baby is not correctly latched on, suckling will not stimulate the breast in the right place and the cycle will be inhibited from the outset and will be unsuccessful.

Positions for breastfeeding

Choose a warm, comfortable and peaceful place in which to feed your baby. Remember not to lean forward and down to your baby but to bring the baby up to you; this will prevent back and neck discomfort and dragging or pulling of the breast tissue, which could cause trauma and pain to your nipples. Guide and direct your baby's head towards the breast very gently – never force the head towards the breast as the baby will resist and may tug or pull at your breast.

Football-hold (clutch) position

The football-hold is a comfortable position in the early days, especially if you have had a cesarean. Tuck your baby securely under your arm on the same side as the breast from which you intend to feed. Bring her up to the breast with her tummy facing your body. Support her neck and shoulders and gently guide her mouth to your nipple.

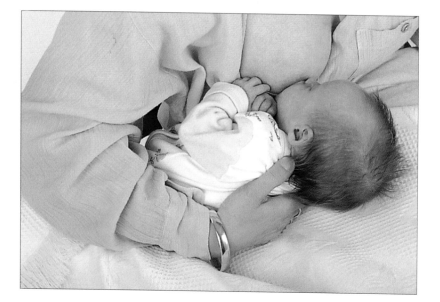

Lying position

Use this position once breastfeeding is well established and your baby is latching on correctly. Lie on your side with one pillow behind your back and another beneath your head and shoulders. Place your baby next to you, with the baby's tummy facing your body. Draw the baby close to you and support the neck and shoulders. Place a receiving blanket or small towel behind the baby to keep him or her as close to you as possible. Nurse from the lower breast.

Madonna (sitting) position

Sit comfortably and well supported in a chair or on a bed with your feet firmly on a flat surface to reduce strain on your back. Place pillows in your lap to bring your baby up to the level of your breast. Cradle your baby's neck in the crook of your arm on the same side as the breast from which you intend to nurse. Your baby should lie facing you with the tummy touching yours. Let the rest of the body curl snugly around yours but keep the head in line with the rest of the body. Use your opposite arm to guide the baby's head gently to your breast.

Slowing down your milk flow
At times your milk flow may be too rapid for your baby to deal with. To help solve this problem lie on your back with your head and shoulders slightly raised on a pillow. Place your baby across your body with head and shoulders supported by your hand. This position forces the baby to suck against gravity and slows down the intake of milk. It also prevents the milk from shooting out to the back of the baby's throat and choking him or her. After two or three days your milk flow will slow down and you will be able to nurse in one of the other positions.

Nursing twins
You may decide to nurse twins one at a time using any of the positions described above, or you may choose to nurse them simultaneously using either the Madonna (sitting) position or the football-hold (clutch) position, which are both suitable for nursing twins. You may also combine them by placing one baby in a football-hold position and the other in the Madonna position; they will then be lying across your body, with the feet of the one baby touching the head of the other.

Offering your baby the breast

Adopt your chosen position for feeding. Your baby's head should be tilted backwards with the chin toward the breast. Cupping your whole breast with your hand and not just the nipple, gently stroke the baby's cheek with your nipple. The rooting reflex will cause the baby's head to turn towards the nipple and the mouth to open. Tease your baby in this way until the mouth is wide open and then quickly put the nipple inside the mouth. Aim your nipple in the direction of the back of the hard palate. Your nipple should be drawn so far back into the baby's mouth that it touches the soft palate. The baby's jaws will compress the reservoirs behind your areola, causing the milk to squirt into his or her mouth. Make sure that your baby's tongue is placed under the nipple and areola and not on top of it.

Checking that your baby is correctly latched on

Correct positioning and latching on of the baby on the breast are vital and will prevent problems such as failure of the baby to thrive, sore nipples, breast engorgement and inadequate milk supply.

Breastfeeding should not hurt – if it does there is something wrong. Make sure that you are in a comfortable position at all times. There should be no friction of the tongue or gum on the nipple and no movement of the breast tissue in and out of the baby's mouth. If there is, you may need to take your baby off the breast and try again. Remember that babies breastfeed, they do not nipple feed! Check that:

- your baby's mouth is wide open and the lower lip is curled outward;
- you can see the baby's tongue protruding over the lower lip;
- the baby is close to the breast and is not dragging on it;
- as the baby suckles, the jaw muscles move in the region of the ears, and the ears 'wiggle';
- you can hear the baby swallowing and see milk at the corners of the mouth;
- if at all, more of the areola can be seen protruding from the upper lip and less from the lower lip;
- your baby is relaxed and contented – not stiff, tense and frustrated.

When your baby is latched on correctly (top) the mouth should be wide open with the lower lip curled back. The baby should come off the breast spontaneously when he or she has had enough. However, if you do need to remove the baby from the breast, simply place the tip of your little finger inside the baby's mouth and gently break the vacuum as the jaws open (bottom).

Timing, duration and frequency of feedings

As some babies take in milk quicker than others, it is impossible to say how much time your baby should spend at the breast. Instead, watch for signs of satiation, as this will ensure that you do not take your baby off the breast before he or she is ready. Babies normally suck rapidly at the beginning of a feeding and much slower as the richer, fattier milk comes in towards the end of the feeding. If you take your baby off the breast too soon, the baby will have received volume from the foremilk but not enough calories from the hindmilk and will not be satisfied for long. A baby for whom this is a problem will cry for a feeding in a very short while, leading the mother – who does not realize that she has taken her baby off the breast too soon – to question the 'quality' and quantity of her milk supply.

Most doctors and midwives will advise you to let your baby finish nursing at one breast before burping and changing to the other breast. This allows the baby to receive both the foremilk and the hindmilk from a breast. On the second breast the baby may take only a little milk before being satisfied or may finish that breast as well. A good indication that your baby is receiving an adequate supply of breast milk is six to ten wet diapers in a 24-hour period. Start the next feeding on the same breast that the previous feeding finished on.

Flexi-feeding is recommended: some babies will nurse more frequently than others, every two to three hours, and others will go longer between feedings, lasting three to four hours. Growth spurts occur at about one week, three weeks, six weeks and three months of age, and your baby will want to nurse more than usual for a few days. It is imperative to 'go with the flow' and nurse more often. At the end of these growth spurts the baby will usually reward you by doing something new that he or she has not done before. The extra nursing demands during these growth spurts often cause mothers to doubt the quality of their milk supply; however, they actually are a sign that your baby is thriving and is developing normally.

If you have inverted nipples discuss this with your doctor. Babies latch onto the areola and not the nipple so it is still perfectly possible to breast-feed even if you suffer from this problem.

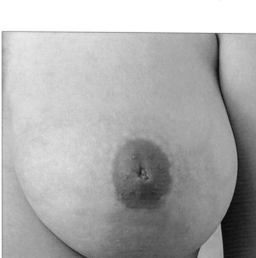

Breast care

- Always wear a well-supporting bra that does not squeeze or flatten your nipples. Towards the end of your pregnancy and for a while after delivery it may be necessary to wear a bra while you sleep.
- Do not scrub your nipples or try to toughen them by applying things like alcohol: this may cause them to crack.
- Avoid using soap on your nipples as it is very drying and washes away the natural oils of the breast. If the nipple appears dry, apply nipple-moisturizing cream.
- If your breasts leak milk, use nursing pads tucked inside the cup of your bra to avoid discomfort and the embarrassment of stained clothes (nylon, in particular, stains badly). Both washable and disposable nursing pads are readily available.

Expressing milk

You may need to express milk to relieve engorgement of the breast, to reduce the pressure of the milk flow or to collect milk for storing for a later feeding when breastfeeding is not possible (for example, if your baby is premature or your nipples are severely cracked, or you are leaving the baby with a babysitter for the evening). Remember that your baby is the best pump, and the amount of milk you manage to express is no indication of the amount that your baby gets out. If your reason for expressing is that your baby has nursed from one breast only and the other is uncomfortable, express only enough milk to make you feel comfortable. Do not drain the breast until it is soft as your body will make this same amount of milk for the next feeding and you could end up being even more uncomfortable.

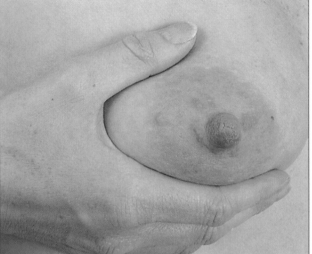

To express breast milk *cup your breast and then press back towards your chest, gently squeezing the areola.*

Many women prefer to express milk using a breast pump rather than manually. Breast pumps are not expensive to buy, and may be available from your doctor. Always express after rather than before a feeding, into a sterilized, non-glass container (the macrophages in breast milk stick to glass and so a lot of 'goodness' will be left behind in a glass container). The expressed milk can be stored for later use.

- Always sterilize the utensils that you will use for expressing.
- Cover and cool expressed breast milk before adding it to stored milk.
- Breast milk may be stored in the fridge for up to 24 hours, or frozen in sterilized ice trays for up to 3 months.
- When reheating frozen milk, stand the bottle in a jug of warm water to defrost. Don't microwave the milk as this destroys much of its nutritional value.
- Discard unused stored milk.

It is essential to keep *bottle-feeding equipment scrupulously clean. This can be done in the dishwasher.*

GUIDE TO BOTTLE-FEEDING

One of the great advantages of bottle-feeding is that your partner can be involved in feeding, enhancing the relationship between him and your new baby. Encourage this as it will be good for all of you, but discourage people other than family members from feeding your newborn as this may make the baby feel confused and insecure. Do not listen to anyone who tries to make you feel guilty if you have decided to bottle-feed. You can get as much satisfaction from feeding your baby as any mother who breastfeeds does.

Bottle-feeding equipment

♦ 6–8 8-oz plastic bottles with caps and dust covers
♦ 2 4-oz plastic bottles with caps and dust covers, for juice (optional)
♦ 6–8 nipples
♦ Accurate measuring spoon (comes with formula)
♦ Formula powder
♦ Funnel (optional)
♦ Bottlebrush
♦ Bottle warmer (optional)

Choose a formula suitable for your baby's needs – as she grows older you will have to change to a richer formula.

Nipples
There are several differently shaped nipples on the market, although orthodontic nipples seem to be the most popular. Buy one nipple at a time to try out on your baby and to see which one he or she prefers.

Choosing a formula
If you have decided to formula-feed, the baby will be given a formula in the hospital appropriate to a newborn. As the baby grows older it will be necessary to change to a richer formula. If you are unsure about what formula to choose, or if the baby develops a sensitivity towards a certain formula, seek advice from your pediatrician. Watch out for any signs of allergies or constipation.

Making up a feeding
Follow the instructions on the can exactly. Use cooled, boiled water. Never put the powder into very hot water as this causes constipation. Make up enough feedings for a 24-hour period only, and discard any prepared feedings after this time is up. Check the temperature of the formula against your wrist, not in your mouth. Beware of bottle warmers – do not leave the bottle in a warmer for longer than ten minutes as this encourages the growth of bacteria. In addition, formula kept warm for a long time will lose much of its nutritional value and may cause constipation. Do not reheat your baby's bottles as this too may encourage constipation and colic.

How much to give?
Use the instructions on the can as a guide. You should never add more formula to the water than specified, but you may want to offer your baby more feedings than the can recommends. Babies differ in their feeding habits and needs. Check the baby's weight gain (see page 133) to see whether he or she is thriving, and flexi-feed to accommodate your baby's individual needs.

Hygiene and sterilization

- When preparing bottles always wash your hands and have a spotlessly clean working area.
- Keep prepared bottles in the fridge.
- Do not keep milk warm for too long.
- Always discard leftover milk.
- Do not use the microwave oven to heat bottles of formula. Not only is this dangerous as they may get too hot, but the microwaves destroy much of the formula's nutritional value.
- Both bottle and nipple should be rinsed thoroughly as soon as possible after a feeding.
- Rub a little coarse salt into the nipple to remove milky build-up.
- Once cleaned and rinsed, both bottle and nipple must be sterilized by boiling them for 10 minutes or by using the dishwasher.
- If necessary, rinse sterilized items with boiling water not tap water.
- Sterilize your bottlebrush and all other accessories from time to time.

Positions for feeding

Position yourself as described for breastfeeding on page 124. Hold your baby as close to you as possible, while cuddling, smiling and talking. Never prop your small baby up and leave him or her sucking at the bottle while unattended. Hold the baby in such a position that you can comfortably angle the bottle to keep the neck full of milk – this minimizes swallowing of air.

When feeding your baby hold the bottle so that the neck is full of milk (below right) – this helps to prevent your baby swallowing air as she drinks. A distinct advantage of bottle-feeding is that your partner will be able to share this task, enhancing the relationship between him and your new baby (below left).

Make sure *that you burp your baby during and after every feeding (this is something that close family members such as grandmothers can help you to do). You may adopt any position which suits you, including laying your baby across your lap: place the baby's tummy down on a pillow across your knees. Gently rub up the baby's back with one hand as you support the head with the other.*

You may prefer *to burp your baby sitting up: hold the baby in a sitting position in your lap. Support the baby's chin with one hand; with the palm of the other hand gently but firmly rub the baby's back in an upward direction.*

WEIGHT GAIN

The best way to check that your baby is thriving is to check his or her weight gain regularly. This is usually done by your pediatrician at well-baby checkups. Babies lose about 10% of their birth weight in the first few days, but should regain their birth weight within ten to 18 days. A breastfed baby does not necessarily gain weight at the same rate as a formula-fed baby, who may gain more (the average weight gain for a breastfed baby is 4–9 oz or 120–250 g per week). Note that continuing weight gain is more important than the amount of weight gained. Plot your baby's weight on a chart (available from your pediatrician). Remember that fluctuations will occur because of things like weighing inaccuracies, but that it is the overall pattern of growth that is important.

ESTABLISHING GOOD SLEEPING HABITS

Newborn babies sleep a lot, but not for long stretches at a time. A newborn will sleep 12–20 hours out of 24 hours. This sounds like a lot, but the sleep cycles are short and frequent. It is a good idea to establish good sleeping habits from the beginning, but don't be too rigid. Babies are born with different personalities and temperaments and this will affect their sleep patterns. Make sure that you put your baby to sleep on his or her back, as it reduces the risks of crib death (Sudden Infant Death Syndrome, or SIDS).

Once your baby has established good sleeping habits he or she will usually be able to sleep at any time, anywhere.

Helpful hints

◆ A hungry baby will start to whimper and eventually cry loudly if no response is forthcoming from the mother. Try not to let your baby get this distressed as he or she will find it difficult to go back to sleep.

◆ Do not put on any bright lights during the night feedings as your baby will wake up more fully.

◆ Do not stimulate or play with him in the night when you want to get back to bed as quickly as possible. Keep any cooing, smiling or laughing for the daytime.

◆ Do not keep the house abnormally quiet at night. A little normal household noise is acceptable and babies often sleep better if there are the comforting sounds of the home around them.

◆ Put something that has your smell on it in the crib – your baby will feel more secure and sleep better.

◆ Swaddling (wrapping the baby up tightly in a receiving blanket) may help your baby feel more secure.

◆ If your baby falls asleep in your arms or while being breastfed, he or she will usually settle into deep sleep very quickly when placed in the crib.

Cord care

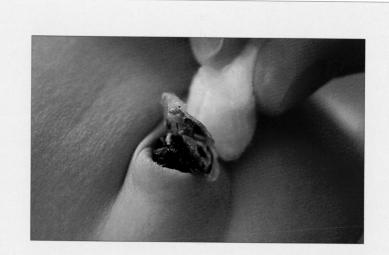

It is important to take good care of the cord after each bath and diaper change. Clean around the base of the cord with alcohol every time you change the diaper, and expose it to the air as much as possible. Surgical baby wipes, available from your doctor, are ideal for keeping the cord clean. Alternatively, dab alcohol onto a cotton ball, and pat it onto and all around the cord stump. Then dip a clean cotton swab into the alcohol and clean around the ridge of the stump, getting right down to the root of the cord. It is normal for the cord to bleed a little before it falls off, so don't let this worry you. However, if the skin around the cord looks hot and angry and has an offensive smell, contact your pediatrician (infection is unlikely if you clean the cord with every diaper change). The cord will usually fall off after 7–14 days. Take care not to cover the cord stump when you put on a diaper.

BATH BASICS

Newborns do not need to be bathed every day, although you will need to clean their bottoms very well at least once a day. A thorough sponge bath will do on the days between baths. This involves cleaning the face and the cord and genital area with a sponge instead of immersing the whole body in water.

Golden rules:

- Keep all your bath supplies within easy reach and make sure that the height of the work area (table and bath) is comfortable – equivalent to the height of your kitchen counter tops.
- Never leave your baby unattended for any reason on a high surface or in the water, even if using a bath aid. Babies, including newborns, wriggle and move around a lot and may easily fall or slip under the water.
- Make sure that the room temperature is comfortable.
- The water must not be too hot or cold – it should be 95.8–97° F (39–40° C). Check the temperature of the water with your elbow or wrist – not your hand.
- Never use washcloths, which harbor bacteria, to wash your baby's face and bottom. Instead, use clean cotton balls.
- Bathe your baby before feeding. However, if the baby starts to cry due to obvious hunger, don't wait until you have finished the bath: wrap the baby up and begin feeding her immediately.

Wrap the baby in a towel and clean the face first, using only clean water and three large cotton balls. Clean the eyes one at a time, wiping from the inside of the eye out towards the ear, and using a separate cotton ball for each eye. Clean behind and over the outside of the ears. Do not place anything inside the ear canal as it is easy to damage the eardrum. Don't insert anything into the nostrils to clear them as this is likely to push any mucus back into the nose.

When you have finished cleaning the baby's face and while still snugly wrapped in the towel, tuck the baby under your arm in the 'football-hold' position (see page 124). Leaning over the bath, gently but firmly wash the hair with a mild shampoo. Rinse off and dry well, especially if he or she has a lot of hair.

Lay the baby down on an opened towel and 'soap' well, front and back, with bath gel or soap, getting into all the creases in the neck and groin area.

If you have an uncircumcised baby boy don't pull back the foreskin, but gently and carefully remove the waxy substance beneath it with a cotton ball. If your baby has been circumcised see page 138.

The baby's skin will be extremely slippery so you must grasp the baby securely to place him or her in the bath: slide your hands under the body and grasp the arm and leg on the opposite side. Lower the baby into the water and rinse off all soap or gel.

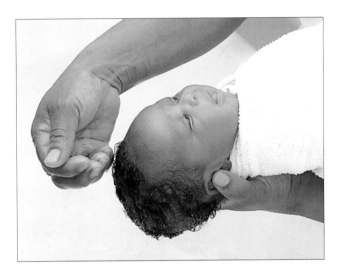

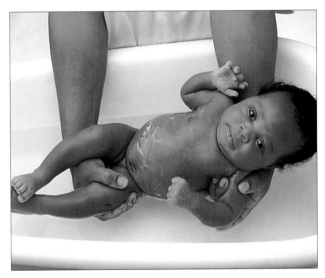

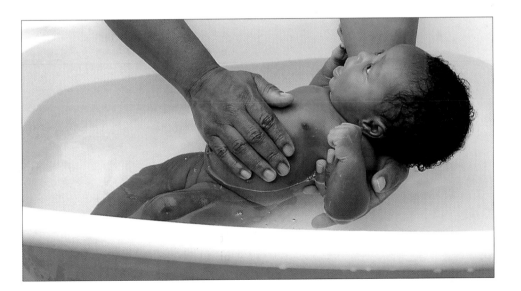

Cover her ears *with your fingers when you rinse your baby's hair and face (top). When you lift to put the baby in the bath water, slide your hands under the body, grasp the arm and leg on the opposite side and hold firmly but gently (middle). Most babies are relaxed and happy in the bath water (left).*

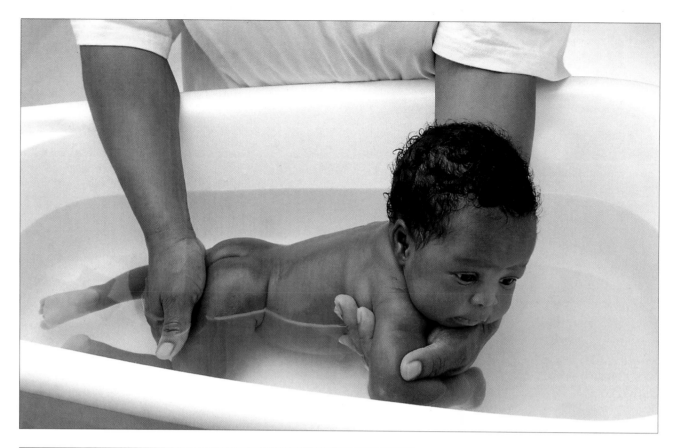

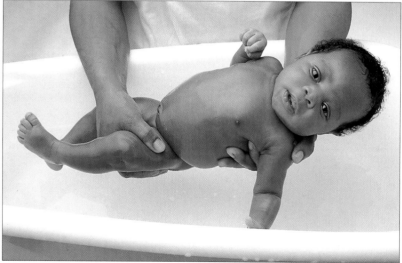

Turn your baby onto the tummy and let him or her kick if there is any crying (top). When you lift your baby out of the water grasp firmly and hold the arm and leg as you did when you put your baby into the bath (above).

If your baby cries even after being put into warm water, turn the baby around to face downwards, still supporting the baby with your hands. Ideally, the bath should be deep enough for the baby to kick freely.

When finished, lift the baby out of the bath holding a leg and an arm as you did to put the baby in the water. Wrap the baby in a towel.

Lay the baby on the table, apply bath oil if you wish to, and dry well, especially in all the creases. Clean the cord now (see page 134).

Don't apply unnecessary creams to the body as the baby may have sensitive skin. Use baby powder with caution: place a small amount of powder on a large cotton ball and rub it onto the back and chest once you have put on an undershirt. Never powder the diaper area as the powder combines with diaper rash cream to form little balls that will chafe the skin.

Dress the baby quickly but gently, wrap well in a receiving blanket, and feed or put the baby down to sleep.

DIAPER KNOW-HOW

As a new parent you can look forward to many diaper changes in the first two to three years of your baby's life. Although you may feel awkward in the beginning, you will soon master this task. You may find it convenient to lay out a special place in your home for diaper changing. Make sure you have all that you need on hand: a clean disposable or regular diaper and pins if necessary, warm water or cleansing lotion, cotton balls and a diaper rash cream containing zinc oxide. Be sure to change your baby's diaper frequently to keep him or her comfortable and to reduce the chances of diaper rash developing.

CHANGING A DIAPER

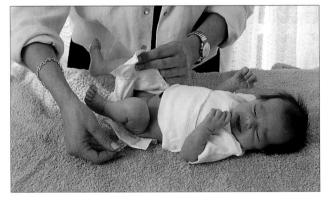

Place your baby *on his or her back and remove the dirty diaper.*

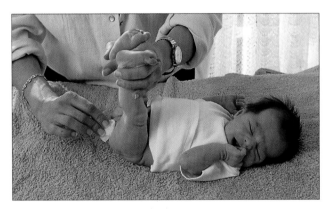

Using warm water *or cleansing lotion and cotton balls, wipe your baby's bottom from the front back towards the anal area. Be sure to clean thoroughly inside the folds of skin around the groin.*

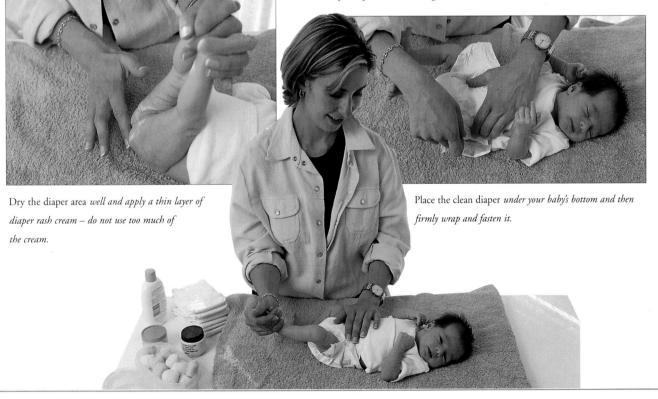

Dry the diaper area *well and apply a thin layer of diaper rash cream – do not use too much of the cream.*

Place the clean diaper *under your baby's bottom and then firmly wrap and fasten it.*

FOLDING A DIAPER

Fold *the diaper in four as shown.*

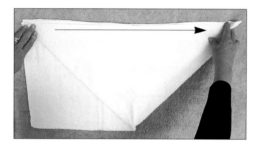

Lift the top corner *and pull it slowly across in a straight line until it flattens out to form a triangular top section.*

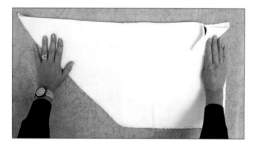

Flip the diaper *over so that the triangular section is underneath.*

Fold the vertical *side of the diaper over once and flatten.*

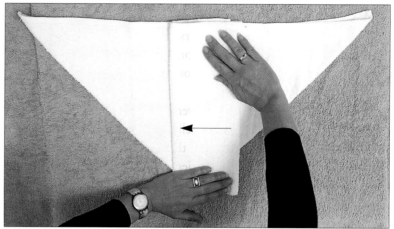

Fold this strip *over once again so that it lies in the center of the triangle-shaped folded diaper. This method of folding gives you a thickly padded inner segment suitable for both girls and boys, but particularly for boys.*

Diaper rash

Always change a wet diaper as soon as you can. Urine is broken down by bacteria that are present on the baby's skin to form ammonia, which burns and is responsible for the redness of the skin. In persistent cases, diaper rash can be serious, with painful ulceration and inflammation. Do not try to cure diaper rash with soap and water. Use baby lotion, or special zinc oxide cream. Do not dress the baby in plastic pants. Leave the baby without a diaper whenever possible so that air can circulate around the diaper area.

CIRCUMCISION: YES OR NO?

Circumcision is the surgical removal of the foreskin, the piece of skin covering the tip of the penis. Circumcision of the newborn is not recommended today, unless it is requested by parents for religious reasons. It is not necessarily healthier or more hygienic and rarely needs to be done for medical reasons (very seldom are boys born with a small opening in the foreskin that might interfere with the passage of urine). Complications ranging from the minor to the serious can also occur, such as bleeding, infection and trauma to the head of the penis. If circumcision is necessary for a medical reason later in life, the operation is best performed by a surgeon in hospital after the patient has been given a general anesthetic. Discuss the decision of whether to circumcise your baby with your pediatrician.

SURVIVAL STRATEGIES FOR NEW MOTHERS

◆ Look after yourself both physically and emotionally. You will be no good to anyone if you do not feel good yourself.

◆ Keep the channels of communication with your partner open and nurture your relationship – both you and your baby will rely on your partner's support and understanding.

◆ Trust your instincts! No one will ever know your baby as well as you do.

◆ You may well be inundated with well-meant advice. Sift through it to choose those bits that suit you and discard the rest.

◆ Remember that mothering gets easier with time! While you may feel that you will never sleep again, this intense period of new motherhood will be over quicker than you realize as your baby grows up, and you adjust and settle into a routine.

◆ Accept any offers of help that come your way. Ask trusted friends and family members to babysit while you go out for half an hour, even if only for a walk around the block. Friends can also help by doing some grocery shopping for you or preparing a frozen meal or two.

◆ Try to develop friendships with other new parents – it helps keep the hard work of parenting in perspective to know that others are going through very similar experiences.

◆ Take the phone off the hook and hang a 'Do Not Disturb' sign on the front door when you are sleeping or feeding your baby.

◆ Give up all unnecessary household chores in the beginning, and don't worry about keeping your house in perfect order.

◆ Don't compare yourself or your baby to others – many people 'whitewash' their pregnancy, birthing and early mothering experiences and may inadvertently make you feel inadequate.

◆ Continue to read and attend educational talks about parenting and related subjects. Make sure that you continue to make informed decisions.

◆ Remember that all this hard work is a labor of love and your baby will bring you untold rewards and joy.

Enjoy the first few months of your baby's life – this precious time will pass faster than you can imagine.

INDEX

References allude to both text and illustrations.

Published by Lowell House

A division of NTC/Contemporary Publishing Group, Inc.

4255 West Touhy Avenue, Lincolnwood, Illinois 60646-1975 U.S.A.

First published in 1998 by
New Holland Publishers (UK) Ltd
London • Cape Town • Sydney • Auckland

24 Nutford Place
London W1H 6DQ
United Kingdom

80 McKenzie Street
Cape Town 8001
South Africa

Level 1, Unit 4, 14 Aquatic Drive
Frenchs Forest, NSW 2086
Australia

Unit 1A, 218 Lake Road
Northcote, Auckland
New Zealand

10 9 8 7 6 5 4 3 2 1

ISBN 0-7373-0413-8

All photographs by Lisa Trocchi with the exception of pages 27, 67, 68 and 69 (Craig Fraser).

Reproduction by Hirt & Carter Cape (Pty) Ltd

Printed and bound in Malaysia by Times Offset (M) Sdn Bhd